HAL CLEMENT

by

Donald M. Hassler

Starmont Reader's Guide 11

BORGO PRESS / WILDSIDE PRESS

www.wildsidepress.com

This book is dedicated to my wife, Sue Hassler

Library of Congress Cataloging in Publication Data

Hassler, Donald M.
    Hal Clement.

    (Starmont reader's guide, ISSN 0272-7730 ; 11)
    Bibliography: p.
    Includes index.
    1. Clement, Hal, 1922-   --Criticism and interpre-
tation. I. Title. II. Series.
PS3505.L646Z69 1982b   813'.54   83-8709
ISBN 0-916-73227-4

DONALD M. HASSLER is currently the Director of Experimental Programs in the Honors and Experimental College at Kent State University, where he is also Professor of English. He has published widely on science fiction and on British literature, particularly two book-length studies of the 18th-century precursor of science fiction, Erasmus Darwin.

CONTENTS

CANON AND CHRONOLOGY

This is the first book-length critical account of the work of Hal Clement, one of the most highly respected writers of hard science fiction; the following chronology and the introductory chapter will prepare the way for a study of the substantial body of fiction he has published to date.

1922	Born May 30, 1922, at Somerville, Massachusetts. Son of Harry Clarence Stubbs (an accountant) and Marjorie Sidney White (a teacher).
1932	Began to read science-fiction pulps.
1934	Entered Boy Scouts in which he was active both as a boy and as an adult; told stories such as Campbell's "Who Goes There" at campfires.
1936-39	High School education at an excellent technical high school in Cambridge, Massachusetts.
1939-43	Earned an undergraduate astronomy degree at Harvard as a commuter student living at home; wrote "a couple of articles" for *Sky and Telescope*, which was published then at Harvard Observatory.
1941	Sold first science-fiction story "Proof" to John Campbell; it appeared in the June 1942 issue of *Astounding Science Fiction*.
1942	Enlisted in the Air Force in the summer but was permitted to finish Harvard before entering active duty; attended his first science-fiction convention in Boston.

1943-45	Served as B-24 copilot and pilot with the Air Force in Europe; stationed at Norwich and Shipton in England; flew 35 bombing missions.
1943	Made a trip to New York City while in basic training at Atlantic City and met John Campbell for the first time; Campbell suggested idea for story "Technical Error" that became his first cover story in the January 1944 issue of *Astounding Science Fiction*.
1947	Earned Masters degree in Education at Boston University.
1947-49	Taught secondary school in Worchester, Massachusetts.
1949	Began teaching at Milton Academy in Milton, Massachusetts, where he has continued to teach until the present time except for a two-year return to active duty in the Air Force.
1950	*Needle* (novel)
1951-53	Recalied to active duty with his Air Force Reserve Unit; served as Technical Instructor at the Special Weapons School at Sandia Air Force Base in New Mexico. After he returned to Milton Academy, he continued as an Air Force Reserve Officer in a public information unit and delivered many talks about the space program.
1952	Married Mary Elizabeth Myers.
1953	*Iceworld* (novel); birth of son George Clement
1954	*Mission of Gravity* (novel); birth of son Richard Myers
1955	Won second place in the International Fantasy Award for *Mission of Gravity* behind Edgar Pangborn's *A Mirror for Observers*. It is ironic that this is the only major award in science fiction for Clement whose work is so highly spoken of and highly regarded.
1956	*The Ranger Boys in Space* (novel)
1957	*Cycle of Fire* (novel); published his only collaboration "Planet for Plunder" with Sam Merwin, Jr., in *Satellite Magazine; From Outer Space* (reissue of *Needle*)
1958	Outlined basic idea for *The Nitrogen Fix* in a talk at Stone Hill College.
1959	Birth of daughter Christine.
1960	Published talk "Some Notes on Xi Bootis System" for the 18th World Science-Fiction Convention in Pittsburgh, Pennsylvania. Earned Masters degree in Chemistry at Simmons College.
1963	*Close to Critical* (novel)
1964	*Natives of Space* (three novelettes)
1969	*Small Changes* (short fiction); reissued as *Space Lash*; at the urging of the New England Science Fiction Association of which he had been a charter member, he began the gathering and editing work on a book about first flights to the Moon.
1970	*First Flights to the Moon* (edited with foreword, notes, and an essay by Clement)
1971	*Star Light* (novel). Nominated for Hugo Award.
1973	*Ocean on Top* (novel)
1976	*Left of Africa* (novel)
1978	*Through the Eye of a Needle* (novel)
1979	*The Best of Hal Clement* (short fiction)
1980	*The Nitrogen Fix* (novel)
1981	Latest guest-of-honor appearance at a science-fiction convention in Albany, New York.

Hal Clement

BIOGRAPHIC AND THEMATIC INTRODUCTION

Few critics have taken science fiction as seriously as they might. [1] Not only the popular literature of Comic Books themselves, which is another genre, but the novels and stories of modern science fiction that date back to the pulp magazines of the late twenties and thirties constitute a popular entertainment that also contains significant meaning for our time. Although all science fiction can be considered part of fantasy fiction since the narratives are alien to the world as we know it, the writers of what has come to be known as "hard" science fiction hold a dominant interest in the methods and findings of modern science. Hard science-fiction writers will often say they are more interested in science and technology than in literature. In addition, many of these writers who were raised on the commercially sensitive, often struggling, pulp magazines are proud to say they turn out fictions primarily for money. Conversely, many hard science-fiction writers grew up in the fan organizations promoted by the pulps; and they thrived on the fascination inherent in popular mechanics and popular science so that science fiction for them is essentially fun, a hobby and a paying enterprise at the same time. The result of these various and often contradictory circumstances is a growing body of literature that does not claim to be serious literature, that is produced for commercial reasons and for fun, that seems to be, in short, precisely deserving of the neglect that students of serious literature have visited upon it. In this study, I will explore the work of Hal Clement, a major hard science-fiction writer, to suggest the complexity and promise of his themes, the intricacy and appropriateness of his tonal effects, and the overall significance of his fictions.

Clement, whose real name is Harry Clement Stubbs, is typical of the hard science-fiction writer. He entered Harvard College in 1939 soaked in science fiction and intending to major in astronomy. He wrote the story that was supposed to be his first published fiction late in his sophomore year or the summer following; he cannot remember exactly when except that he does remember writing an earlier piece of science fiction, the title forgotten, that has remained unpublished. [2] "Proof," his second story and the first published, is a reasoned speculation told from the point of view of a life form evolved within the gaseous interior of the Sun that cannot imagine metals and other elements existing in a solid state. This extrapolation seems comically absurd both from the point of view of characters who cannot conceive of solids and from the point of view of the reader who cannot conceive of the characters, but the tale is presented as logically plausible and hence science fiction of the hard kind. The story was accepted by John W. Campbell, editor of *Astounding Science Fiction* which was the leading pulp magazine for hard science fiction, in October 1941 and appeared the following June in an issue with a cover story that was to become part of Isaac Asimov's *Foundation Trilogy*. [3] At the time he was writing "Proof" and his other early stories, Clement was also writing articles for *Sky and Telescope* and studying with the solar expert Donald Menzel. [4] He recalls his concern that Menzel and his other teachers might disapprove of science fiction, and so at the suggestion of his sister he signed his stories with his middle name, Clement. He later found out that Menzel himself had tried to write science fiction. By that time, Hal Clement had become a familiar name in the pages of *Astounding*.

His work as a man of science has continued steadily since those early days at the Harvard Observatory. In the summer of 1942, he enlisted in the Army Air Force Reserve but was allowed to complete his undergraduate degree in Astronomy before beginning pilot training. Clement flew thirty-five bombing missions over Europe as a copilot and pilot on a B-24, and his interest in meteorology resulted in several stories written while he was based in England. Although he had taken one semester of "Writing" at Harvard and was himself a published author (his first cover story, "Technical Error," appeared in the January 1944 *Astounding*), Clement has said that he never considered writing realistic fiction about his war experiences. [5] Following the war, he set out to write science fiction and to teach science. He earned a Masters in Education from Boston University in 1947, taught secondary school in Worcester, Massachusetts, and in 1949 earned an appointment as science teacher at the exclusive Milton Academy (T. S. Eliot's prep school) in Milton, Massachusetts. Except for two additional years as a technical instructor at Sandia Air Force Base in New Mexico during the Korean War when he flew a little more, Clement has continued to teach at Milton and to write science fiction. He is a great supporter of NASA and served in a public information unit giving speeches about the space program until his retirement from the Air Force. He has written some non-fiction on education and for science textbooks, and at the urging of the New England Science Fiction Association, probably the most sophisticated fan organization in the country, he edited a collection of stories, including his own non-fiction history, dealing with the first manned lunar landing entitled *First Flights to the Moon* (1970). [6] His most consistently excellent work, however, has been a growing body of science-fiction stories and novels. By the end of 1980, he had published eleven novels, two of them marketed as juveniles, and three collections of shorter pieces.

The income from this body of work, in a field that has from the start been commercially alert, must have been considerable. Clement has said that the money from his writing essentially has put his three children through college. [7] But even though Clement has made money at his writing and even though he is currently highly respected by fans of hard science fiction, he consistently and almost naively maintains that he writes primarily for fun. He says that though he knows he is a good storyteller, he is not a literary writer. [8] He says that he enjoys both the storytelling, which he traces back in his own experience to telling other people's stories around Boy Scout campfires in the thirties, and the analytic and quantitative calculations that he works out for each of his fictions prior to writing them down; and if he were to have to choose, he says he enjoys the slide-rule work more than the fiction. [9] In fact, like some enigmatic poets I have known, Clement even bristles at times in a friendly and non-aggressive manner to the suggestion that there might be hidden meanings in his work. He writes in a letter:

> I don't feel competent at psychoanalysis even of myself, and am not aware of any subtle hidden meanings in any of my stories. I write them, generally speaking, for fun—though I suppose my idea of fun would be another handle for the analyst. [10]

Often among science-fiction writers, I think, the sense of competence may protest a bit too much. In fact, recently in a general introduction to the science-fiction writer Isaac Asimov, James Gunn assumes the militantly simple position that this type of literature should not be searched for effects beyond the most obvious effects of plot. Gunn, who is himself an important writer of science fiction as well as one of its critics, explains that his study will include a number of plot summaries'' . . . because what happens is the most important aspect of Asimov's fiction (and most other science ficton), and what happens is revealed in plot.'' [11]

Although I see this critical position as an outgrowth of the "fun and fan" syndrome that has been part of the genre since the early days of the pulps, I see no reason why it should determine the manner in which we must approach the works. Hard science fiction may be an attempt to popularize hard science in which the story outline is the most important communication device, but it also may contain some thematic, imagistic, and even tonal complexities about the meaning of science that are not at first apparent. In this sense, Hal Clement's work may be harder than it seems and harder than he says it is. By all standards of both science and literature, such puzzles of difficulty in reading should make the works even more fun. I grant that little is more silly than the over intellectual academic critic fooling with the real writer, the energetic terrier hardly notice by the substantial Saint Bernard. So although my work no doubt at times will nip at the heels of a large body of fiction, I hope to draw circles around key notions in Clement's work that later may be filled in with more detail. I am looking for the interesting ideas; these are sometimes expressed in plot situations, sometimes in character, image, theme, and tone.

During my recent interview with him, Clement acknowledged that as a seeker after complexities I would enjoy his latest novel, then still in press and published in the fall of 1980; so perhaps *The Nitrogen Fix* is a good place to begin in the exposition of several provocative ideas in Clement's work because it represents the latest product of a consistently thoughtful writing career. [12] Teasing me (the teaser) about the story that I had not yet had the opportunity to read, Clement said:

> I've mentioned already the thing in *The Nitrogen Fix*. The non-human, alien creature is completely sexless, has no sex drive, and I had to find some substitute for this which might reasonably motivate an intelligent being . . . . You'll have some fun with that. A lot of people will have fun psychoanalyzing me on that one. [13]

In this tale, about a future earth, in which genetic engineering intended to enhance agriculture has reduced free oxygen in the atmosphere to a trace, the alien behavior that replaces sex is learning. The prime motivation for alien "Observers" who have been drawn to the earth by the nitrogen buildup in the atmosphere is simply curiosity. The Observers are a hive species, sexless; reproduction is by parthenogenesis. Each individual unit, of which two figure in the novel, can share total communication and memory with the entire species once contact with any other unit has been made. Thus the pooling of knowledge that the aliens do by touching, in a world where science and experimental knowledge are dirty words because of the dirty trick that genetic engineering has played, makes them seem even more alien. Clement's ambiguities about touching here seem more interesting than the mere nervous self-consciousness he expressed that his fiction would not conform to the usual expectations for sex in contemporary fiction. Science fiction, of course, is notoriously devoid of stories with a love interest—with just a few exceptions and Clement is not one. [14] What substitutes in Clement as a magnificent passion is the value of curiosity coupled with serious issues about epistemology, and he knows these are his themes. As the surviving humans in the novel struggle among themselves and, also, struggle to understand the peculiar aliens, the most helpful Observer, who has been named "Bones" since he has no skeleton (irony seems to be everywhere in Clement) tries to comprehend human epistemology:

> Bones was fascinated. Psychology was another totally new field to a mind which had not only never met another intelligent species until now, but had never encountered a different mind in its own. This crowd of *individuals*, cut off from each other except through crude and time-consuming code symbols, was a revelation—a brand new field of knowledge—indeed, a whole set of such fields. It was obvious that the incomplete and distorted picture of the universe transmitted by words would have fantastically unpredictable effects on those minds; the code symbols themselves would probably take the place of the reality they were supposed to transmit much of the time . . . .
>
> It would not occur to Bones for a long time that the Observer's sensory impressions were just as much a coded representation of reality as were human words. So were the molecular patterns which

recorded those impressions, and passed them from one Observer unit to another. The species was a good scientist, but not yet a philosopher. [15]

What interests Clement is not only the nitrogen-based physiology and alien appearance of this character, both of which are fantastic extrapolations from plausible bases hence hard science fiction, but also the puzzles of epistemology that the character encounters. Even though the Observer species can communicate by direct chemical interaction, with the droll analogy to human sexual contact, knowledge for the species is still indirect and thus uncertain. Clement suggests, in other words, that regardless of what symbol system we use to perceive and to communicate we can never be sure exactly what the universe is made of, and his expression of that theme in the Observer species is only his most recent attempt to speculate about a basic epistemological problem. Since knowledge and the communication of knowledge are at best only partially efficient, the means of acquiring knowledge and testing its accuracy are of the utmost importance if the epistemological problem is to be taken seriously. One of Clement's main themes, then, has to do with all the conditions, opportunities, and limitations that govern accurate knowledge about the physical universe.

As the quotation above suggests, this theme is not dry as dust science nor a simple matter; the pursuit of the epistemological problem throughout Clement's work is both serious and provocative. Especially the limitation upon direct revelation of knowledge either by some metaphysical means or by means of depth psychology seems to be a troublesome annoyance in Clement's thinking. This annoyance may manifest itself in his skeptical remarks about psychoanalyzing, and it certainly is the mandate for the patient accumulation of partial knowledge, as through scientific experimentation, since no direct and final knowledge is ever possible. In a story that appeared in *Astounding* in 1947, Clement pits a psychologist against the most advanced computer to unravel finally the nature of mind. The poor psychologist becomes paralyzed in a kind of infinite regress. Near the end of "Answer," Clement's speaker laments:

> Trying to understand perfectly the workings of a brain—with a brain . . . . he'd think, What change is this very thought making in the pattern? and he'd try to include that in his mental picture; and then try to include the change due to *that*, and so on, thinking in smaller and smaller circles. He was conscious enough, I guess, so naturally the stimulants made no difference; and every usable cell of his brain was concentrated on that image, so none of the senses could possibly intrude. Well, he knows now how a brain works. [16]

THEMES RELATED TO KNOWLEDGE

Clement's experimental or Baconian solution to the limitations of knowledge results in what is probably the most well-known characteristic of his work. The creation of a great variety of alien life forms and alien environments, that is a variety of observers, may allow us to escape the plight of the poor psychologist in "Answer" by maintaining a great deal of contact with the outside world. One way to build up a store of partial knowledge, if it cannot be gotten by direct revelation or introspection, is to utilize a lot of curious and potentially intelligent beings. another way is to imagine a lot of variable conditions because as things change more can be learned about what drives the changes—what scientists call thought experiments. Clement is a virtuoso with both kinds of extrapolation in science fiction. His alien life forms are almost all curious creatures as well as shrewd, hence all potential learners. The accumulation of a tremendous amount of data from different points of view is one result. His most well-known aliens are the caterpillar-like Mesklinites from his classic *Mission of Gravity* (1954) who shrewdly learn to overcome their fear of falling, which is no small accomplishment since the variable to immensely high gravity on the fantastic planet Mesklin has evolved life very close to the ground; they even learn from their human visitors the physics of flight. At the same time, of course, Clement's reader learns a lot about Mesklin. [17] Human explorers in Clement stories use intelligent natives to help them learn, and natives as shrewd as the Mesklinites with bodies and home environments as different from Mesklin as Mesklin is from earth use humans in other stories to help them gain knowledge. [18] Clement's vision of cooperating and essentially scientifically-driven life forms throughout the universe is remarkably peaceful and developmental. There seems to be very little tooth and fang competition for life space. The universe seems large enough and long enough for all, and even when mistakes are catastrophic, such as the nitrogen imbalance that makes the earth nearly uninhabitable for oxygen life in his latest novel, the shrewd and accurate manipulation of the natural environment can correct matters. [19] Some of Clement's fictions are modeled after the detective story and a few of his characters, both human and alien, are criminals; but crime is generally overcome in these stories by careful and accurate reasoning. [20]

The really dangerous antagonist in most of Clement's narrative situations, of course, is the universe itself. Here again wide and accurate knowledge about the variability of nature—what will happen given certain conditions—is the answer. It is an answer of probabilities and of variability, in other words, in which the settings or environments in Clement's fictions contribute significant images to the communication of variability. He seems particularly expert in the use of two variables: gravity and temperature. This does sound dull, but what Clement's fictions impress upon the reader are the near infinite possibilities for changing conditions of matter given the closeness or distance from other matter. Planetary environments are, in fact, key characters in Clement's fictions where differences in atmospheric components, in orbit, in mass, in heat all play important parts to entertain and to instruct the reader. And the main message is variety. These conditions are not that far fetched, of course; we experience similar variety of conditions in the various earth environments, in the weather, in the multitude of various life forms on earth. For example, Clement has said that he got the idea for the life conditions on the planet Abyormen in *Cycle of Fire* (1957), where one species evolved for high temperature lives dormant inside another species evolved for low temperature as the planet completes a highly elliptical orbit that drastically changes its average temperature, from an article in *Scientific American* about a form of virus that infests a certain bacillus and then waits through several generations of the bacillus before reappearing. [21]

In spite of the fascination with all this variety in life forms and in environment, there is much about a universe of such plenitude that is unsettling from the human point of view. With much less observational and speculative data at their command, the thinkers of the 18th-century Enlightenment referred to this reaction of disorientation and awe at the vastness and even irregularity of the universe as the effect of the sublime. This effect was often deliberately sought aesthetically to create terror and disorientation as the proper imitation of the vastness of the universe. [22] Another major characteristic in Clement's work is a rendering of this sublime effect of human disorientation. He seems to create the sublime effect frequently with the image of gravity, falling, free fall, circling.

The image may simply have stayed with him after his great success with the extrapolation on variable gravity in *Mission of Gravity*, or it may be that from Newton to the black hole astronomers of our day the mysterious weak force of gravitation has an unavoidable, strong appeal. Who can say for sure why a writer or scientific extrapolator repeats images? But there is no question that, in Clement's fictions of a future world of continually improving science and technology, the peculiarly non-human experience of free fall as well as variable gravity is mentioned and elaborated upon often. From an early juvenile novel in which free fall is seen as a major obstacle to space exploration (*The Ranger Boys in Space*, 1956) through the novels set in various planetary and astral environments, each with variable gravitational forces, to a number of shorter fictions in the last two decades, Clement has continually written about the sensation of falling disorientation that results whenever man leaves his one-gravity earth. From the dramatic fear of falling in the Mesklinites to the nausea of humans in free fall, the experience and image of falling are used by Clement to represent the irony of life's non-adaptability in a variable universe as well as its ability to cope somehow with alien environments and with unfamiliar gravities. Progress proves ironic as it takes man off the familiar "household" of the earth—or as it takes Mesklinites off Mesklin. The computer story, "Answer," that was mentioned above in the discussion of epistemology, contains several sentences that are representative of Clement's matter of fact presentation of the image in a suggestive context. The ultimate computer is housed in a satellite that the questing psychologist, Wren, has to visit off earth:

> Wren had become more or less used to weightlessness on the flight to the station, but its sudden conjunction with so much open space unnerved him for a moment, and he clutched at the arm of the figure drifting beside him . . . .
>
> "I say, don't you spin this place to give centrifugal gravity? I'm still not quite sure of myself without weight." The taller man laughed at the question.
>
> "I suppose we could, though it would be hard to keep the screen spherical with anything like one gravity at its rim. It was decided a long ago that the conveniences derived from spin were far more than offset by the nuisances; you'll be weightless as long as you are here." [23]

In this case, the future technology to create the ultimate computer dictates that people near it remain in the disorientated state of weightlessness. What the computer uncovers is also disorienting as was seen earlier. Partial knowledge and falling are mirrors in Clement of man's limited condition.

A final thematic characteristic that runs throughout Clement's work, which both unifies the work and gives it suggestiveness, is represented in his frequent digressions into the problems of language and communication. If partial knowledge is all we can hope to acquire, then, the perception of that knowledge and the communication of it through languages indicate both the limits of its partiality and its only hope for accumulative gathering. The problems and potentials at the Tower of Babel should always be the concern of fallen and "falling" man. Despite some language clumsiness of its own at times, Clement's work has contained this concern from his latest alien, Bones the Observer, whose problems with language were suggested in the quotation about him/her above, all the way back to "Proof." An alien from the planet Dromm, which Clement has imagined in a secondary way in several novels and that may be awaiting future development in a fiction yet to be written, tells his son, "You mean you . . . let that human girl do all the talking? I'm ashamed of you. You know perfectly well that no chance to learn the use of a new language should ever be missed." [24]

A close attention to the phenomenon of language and to the limitations in communication with language always leads to the expression, and perhaps the understanding of irony. As the reader has no doubt already noticed, Clement likes irony. His titles seem ironic or at least pleasantly ambiguous. *Mission of Gravity* is a grave and epic story with some very droll characters and situations—not exactly mock-epic, but definitely spaced-out epic and yet a very serious story of journeying toward discovery. *The Nitrogen Fix* includes some precise chemical knowledge about "fixing" elements in certain compounds and is also about the survivors' efforts to correct some very serious mistakes in genetic engineering. The short story, "Stuck With It," is about adhesives but also about the limitations again in genetic engineering. Clement's irony is a very literary way of coping with the limitations of partial knowledge, and in spite of his frequent disclaimers to the contrary, he even makes fun sometimes of the science-fiction writer himself—a literary self-consciousness that most critics would never allow this naive genre. Perhaps it is appropriate that the final quotation from his fiction in this brief introduction to Clement's work should be taken from his first published story because even then he expressed well the irony in the situation of the science-fiction writer who dares fantastic speculations to contribute in a limited way to the gradual accumulation of knowledge and ideas. One of the characters made entirely of gaseous matter has listened to his colleague speculate about the totally alien notion of matter existing in a solid state and then recalls that, even though he has suggested the notion originally from some observational data, his colleague has been known to have dabbled perhaps in what we call science fiction:

> I seem to have heard that you have somewhat of a reputation as an entertainer, and you seem quick-witted enough to have woven such a tale on the spot, purely from the ideas I suggested. I compliment you on the tale. [25]

Clement's own tales have been entertaining to many readers over the years and will continue as a substantial portion of the canon of modern science fiction.

But in addition to entertainment, a definite seriousness of intention seems to have determined the gravity and often sublime grandeur of his themes. Epistemology, methods of knowing, variability and possibility as both limitation and method, language as both limitation and method—all express what might be called a world vision that is consistent with the notions of science in our day at the same time that it speculates about the human meanings of science. Finally, the fallings and the ironic circlings are also ways of expressing Clement's vision of the limitations and possibilities in partial knowledge. His stories do not meet the standards and expectations of realistic fiction. His human characterizations are mostly flat and less interesting than his aliens. But there is something finally quite real about the epistemological themes, the sublime images, and the love of knowledge in Clement. I think he may sum up his own fiction best in one sentence from our interview, and the careful qualifications that I have transcribed carefully in the sentence suggest his vision of limited knowledge: "I like to think of things that might happen if our picture of the universe is even moderately accurate." [26] Now we may see through a glass darkly; and for Clement, though it may be had, he will keep looking through that glass because he sees little chance for breaking beyond it.

II.

FICTION OF DETECTION AND IRONY

Needle was Hal Clement's first novel-length fiction and his first fiction to be published in book form although he was well recognized by the time of its appearance in 1950 as an important contributor of hard science fiction to the pages of *Astounding*. It was not unusual for science-fiction writers of the Golden Age to delay book publication until all the fiction had appeared in the pulps, and the market for books of science fiction was really not created until about the time of this first appearance of Clement's work in book form. [27] The original fiction, "Needle," was a 40,000 word serial published in two parts in *Astounding Science Fiction*, April and May, 1949. In fact, Clement has said that a year earlier John Campbell had rejected the first version of the story because the storytelling, as Clement recalls had made the discovery of the alien much too obvious. [28] Later, Clement expanded the serial version by doubling the size of the second part. It was the expanded version that was published as a novel by Doubleday in 1950. Then, in the mid-seventies, Clement returned to the story of the alien Hunter living symbiotically inside humans and wrote a sequel that was published as *Through the Eye of a Needle* (1978).

With a wide experience in reading series-type books, such as detective series or space-opera series, Clement has developed a reluctance to write fictions of his own that are published as series, even though these two "Needle" books are not the only ones he has done successfully, because as he says, "I would build up some background pictures of my own, and then every time I would read another book in the series it destroyed some of my background notions." [29] In other words, in both of these "Needle" novels, a considerable amount of self-conscious reflection has gone into their making—either because of the needed reworking of a first novel or because of the taking up again of a successful situation and cast of characters for a sequel. The result is well-crafted fiction with a good bit of carefully structured irony.

One critic has recently referred to *Needle* as " . . . one of the first successful fusions of the SF and mystery genres." [30] It is no accident that these two genres of popular literature should be linked in Clement's first novel because, in addition to reading eagerly in the science-fiction pulp magazines as he was growing up, Clement read widely in mystery and detective fiction. He was a fan of "The Saint" and read all of the detective stories of Dorothy Sayers. [31] But it was from the pages of *Astounding Science Fiction* in the thirties, before Campbell's editorship, that Clement recalls noticing for the first time the motif of human possession by a virus-like creature that evolved into the central action of his first novel. In tracing this intellectual evolution, he went on to recall an incident that took place after he had just returned from his combat tour with the Air Force and was serving a rest duty at Atlantic City. He was strolling the beach and saw a twelve-year-old boy lying asleep on the sand. He recalls thinking of the comment in Rudyard Kipling's novel *Kim* by the native agent, Hurree Babu, that a boy sleeping in the open was a "fool's trick" and could lead to anything happening to him. [32] The boy sleeping on the beach becomes Robert Kinnaird in *Needle*, and what happens to him is the symbiotic possession by the alien called the Hunter.

In his critical essay on *Needle* in *Survey of Science Fiction Literature*, Walter E. Meyers argues that Clement's creation of this virus-like alien was a specific refutation of L. Sprague de Camp's well-known argument in a nonfiction piece in *Astounding Science Fiction* (May and June, 1939) that intelligent alien life would necessarily have to take a physical form not far removed from the shape and size of the human form. [33] Clement's sympathetic and carefully understood little alien is certainly a thought-experiment refutation of de Camp's narrow anthropocentric argument. But from the beginning of his writing career, as we saw in the discussion of his first published story, Clement has attempted to puzzle out non-anthropocentric bases for intelligent life. This is a key portion of the expression of his theme of variety or variability; and in particular the intellectual roots for *Needle* run much wider and deeper, I think, than a one-shot refutation of de Camp's anthropocentrism—and much deeper than can be fully explored here. From detective fiction to adventure reading to variability, Clement had experienced good preparation to create a provocative and effective first novel.

STRATEGY OF AVOIDANCE

Clement's involvement with the full development of his first novel-length fiction and with the daring concept of alien intelligence that was central to it produced a depth of irony and, what might be called, an imaginative strategy of avoidance that makes the fiction particularly interesting. In fact, he was so convinced of the rightness of his alien that, during the revision of the manuscript for Campbell when he heard of a new story by Theodore Sturgeon with a possession motif, he worried that his idea had been anticipated until he saw the story and knew that Sturgeon had done something different. [34] What Clement did with the alien in *Needle* resulted in his most "Freudian" fiction, notwithstanding his disclaimers noted in the previous chapter, and the alien in this novel can illustrate perhaps most vividly the muted ambiguity in his brand of hard science fiction.

The physical background for the creature is Clement's speculation of a species evolved from viruses, rather than from protozoan cells, into a highly intelligent life form in which only the memory cells are specialized. The other cells are continually changing into various organ forms as need arises, but usually the creature lives most efficiently as a friendly parasite, or symbiont, insinuating its small virus-like cells easily among the larger protozoan-like cells of its host. In the novel, the creature, who is called simply the Hunter, has come to Earth in hot pursuit of a criminal member of its race. When the Hunter, who is a detective by profession among his own kind, adopts as his host the teenager, Bob Kinnaird, they become the best of friends in a delightful and carefully detailed extrapolation on this kind of symbiosis. Phenomenally enough, though, Clement has the enemy or adversary creature adopt Bob's father as its host. The story then unfolds as a tale of detection with a lot of biological extrapolation worked in, but Clement adds very little that is suggestive or psychologically extrapolative about the basic filial conflict that readers of William Wordsworth, James Joyce, or even Thomas Wolfe might expect. It is almost as though Clement invented this story-line and developed it as he did deliberately to demonstrate that hard science fiction extrapolates only from the physical.

As the Hunter gradually makes his presence known to his host, the situation is particularly ripe for the development of Bob's psychological complexity. He is literally two personalities in one, and this is before Clement reveals the conflict between father and son. But the narrative seems to insist that the complexity is all physical, which it is of course, and that Bob's straightforward adolescent mind is the best environment in which the symbiont-host relationship can develop. At the end of chapter five, Clement writes:

> . . . he the Hunter had made an incredibly lucky choice of hosts. A much younger or less well-educated child could not have begun to understand the situation and would have been frightened out of its senses; an adult would probably have headed at top speed for the nearest psychiatrist's office. Bob was old enough to understand at least some of what the Hunter had told him and young enough not to blame the whole thing on subjective phenomena. [35]

Clement's development of the physical relationships is fascinating. The Hunter and Bob learn to communicate. Bob provides the structural form that allows the Hunter to move and to act. The Hunter has the ability of speed healing any time his host suffers illness or injury. The details of all these activities are explained in the novel whereas the subjectively perceived analogues, such as psychosomatic healing or automatic writing, are never more than ghosts in the mind of the reader. The effect is an ironic juggling act between the psyche and the physical phenomena.

This hidden complexity in *Needle* is similar to what a modern structuralist would call the "deconstruction" of avoidance. In addition to the details of subjective phenomena that are given physical explanations in the novel, Clement did construct the story with the basic conflict running between son and father. He did avoid developing this conflict with suggestive imagery or with explicit verbal development; and the effect is a kind of militant coyness. Clement seems to be intending to create, or at least to suggest, a physical (albeit extraterrestrial) explanation for subconscious phenomena that Freud and others have tried to map. Interestingly, Clement has another novelette from the forties in which he provides an extraterrestrial occurrence of vampirism in a small American town, but it has a matter-of-fact and friendly tone that makes it more extrapolation on alien life forms than horror fiction. [36] The tonal effect of Clement's physical explanations for the great, complex ambiguities of the human psyche may be the tone of what one reviewer has termed a grey, filing-cabinet mind. [37] But it is also the thin, hard tone of the vision of epistemological limits referred to in chapter one, and it is the tone of cleverly not telling everything as we shall see in the Mesklinite personality in the next chapter. The end result is irony, wisdom, and the greater knowledge that comes from the ever-widening connection between things rather than from the deep penetration to ultimates.

SEQUEL

Clement's verbal development of irony seems richer and a bit less muted in his sequel about the Hunter and Bob Kinnaird that appeared nearly three decades later under the title *Through the Eye of a Needle* (1978). In this later story of search and detection that Clement claims a fan finally urged him to write, the basic conflict is within the symbiosis itself. For some medical reason, the Hunter's presence is doing damage to his host. Contact must be established with other members of the Hunter's species, who, according to the correct deductions of the Hunter and Bob, must have followed the trail to Earth to get the expert knowledge necessary to stabilize the symbiotic relationship. The Hunter is merely a detective by profession; the other members of his species will include medical experts and xenobiologists. In this later novel, Clement seems to take advantage more often of the inherent opportunities in this symbiosis to suggest complexity of meaning in which what is hidden is often of most importance. The results express the comic ironies of things not being what they seem and the comic possibilities that go with this sort of shrewd detection. For example, the amorphous physiology of the alien is imaged more explicitly than in the earlier novel. The image of an advanced creature with little structural organization as we see it is a droll image. (Most aliens in science fiction are somewhat comic, and the tension between the useful variability of such non-anthropocentrism and its apparent absurdity will be a continual consideration as we encounter more of Clement's aliens.) Now and then Clement realizes the drollery in an explicit verbal way. At one point, the Hunter becomes paralyzed outside his host, and the humans must experiment with first aid for him. Dr. Seever speculates early in chapter eleven:

> I'd say we'd better pour him into something which will give him more exposed surface. [He had been brought in in an iron pipe.] What's his volume—a couple of quarts? A pie plate won't be enough, and I don't suppose separating him among several would be a very good idea. He must have *some* essential continuity to his structure, even if shape doesn't mean anything to him.

I suggested in passing earlier that a valuable way to read much of Clement's apparently simple storytelling so that the underlying and important meanings may be discovered is from the point of view of the modern structuralists and deconstructionists, who look quite simply (and sometimes belaboredly) for the *implied* meanings of a text—much like the new critics proposed three decades before. [38] A core notion of structuralism and, in fact, of any system of language analysis has to do with the inevitable separation between the "sign" in language and the message that is communicated. Since there is a separation, signs can mean different things to different people. In other words, communication is always partial, limited, and suggestive. The situation of the Hunter living in and with Bob does embody some of these language complexities. In *Through the Eye of a Needle*, Clement ventures to verbalize a bit about the complex language relationship although in *Needle* he details the fascinating physiology of how the Hunter teaches Bob to communicate with him which seems to be a combination of automatic writing and nerve manipulation. In an earlier short fiction of Clement's (his second published piece, "Impediment"), the narrative is built around speculation about language in which no "signs" are used at all. The implications of this are fascinating—Clement may have been an early and genuine structuralist in spite of himself. [39] In the symbiosis involving Bob and the Hunter, however, communication does go on within their classic schizophrenic/symbiotic system and among them and the other people around them. Now and then, in *Through the Eye . . .* Clement will detail the process of this three-way communication. It resembles a kind of simultaneous translation with a slight time lag. The implications, of course, are that communication always involves interpretation and is always complex. Things are not quite what they seem although the data are present to create approximate certainties. When the narrator talks early in the sequel novel about Bob's parents believing in his symbiont (by now the possession has left the father, of course), some of this complexity is implied. The quotation is near the beginning of chapter two:

> Under the circumstances they had little choice about believing, and had eventually come to take the Hunter for granted—even addressing him directly at times, though of course their son had to transmit any answers.

MORE THAN HARDY BOYS

Even though both Needle novels do read a little like Hardy Boy books and Clement has been accused more than once of a juvenile flatness in writing, the irony in the symbiotic situation seems too consistently contrived to be ignored by the reader. Bob's parents talking directly to their son's symbiont, which means talking *at* Bob but not *to* him, is more droll than anything to be found in juvenile detective fiction. Usually the sleuthing activity, the mental mode of deduction that a detective uses, is mingled with the drollery. In chapter eleven of *Through the Eye of the Needle,* one of the shrewd teenagers analyzes the behavior of another "possessed" teenager: "I'm still sure, from those slips he made, that he's at the bottom of all this, though." But the scene is the sickroom of the Hunter, and he is lying like a bowl of jelly beside the speakers as this analysis of the discrepancy between appearance and reality takes place. This later novel concludes with a classic scene in which the mystery is unraveled as in traditional detective fiction, and by now the Hunter has recovered and presides over the scene through Bob as clever detective. But the dialogue that Clement writes underlines both the peculiar nature of this detective and the peculiar nature of the detective mode itself. Two questions asked in sequence are pointed at the same ears, but the first question is directed to the Hunter and the second to Bob: "Is that relevant to your Agatha Christie puzzle? Bob, did you ever *feel* this creature *grinning*? [The italics are Clement's]."

Critics who would deny depth to Clement's fiction fail to see the relation between puzzles and irony, and like a true detective or puzzler, Clement never tells all himself. This mode of working by inference and indirection without final knowledge or direct revelation to solve mysteries that usually lead only to further mysteries is exactly how great detectives work. The expectation of mystery and of variability is also what drives the brand of inquisitive, hard science to which Clement subscribes. He does not seem to be seeking final answers or a final synthesis, but rather wants limited answers and, perhaps most of all, the knowledge and power that come from being able to solve puzzles. Such open endedness produces irony. In fact, the irony of living with partial knowledge may be one of the salvations that science fiction and literature in general can offer because they have apparently near infinite variability, not only in our imaginations but also in their own phenomena. The extent to which Hal Clement rises to the occasion of imaging the variability of nature, along with the irony that allows us to accept this variability, is really the central issue of this study of his work. He likes to be coy, cool, and open in his thought, and even though he would never be so dogmatic as to say so, the creation of the Hunter and his fictions expresses effectively this mode of puzzling out infinite mysteries in a somewhat ironic manner.

III.

MESKLIN AND DHRAWN: FORWARD WITH FEAR

In discussing his numerous memories of John Campbell, the editor who encouraged most the kind of hard science fiction that Clement wanted to write, Clement said that Campbell found it difficult ''to believe that anyone could write a false report.'' [40] This gullible side of Campbell that led him now and then to believe in speculative concepts that many other hard science-fiction writers could never accept is alien to the Hume-like skepticism built into the ironic, detective mode of character that peoples most of Clement's fictions. Add to this shrewdness and testiness of thought, which neither tells all nor has confidence that others tell all, a massive variability or difference in unusual planetary environments and you have the narrative elements that proved particularly valuable for Clement in the novels following *Needle*. In between, he did publish a second novel, *Iceworld* (1953), in which Earth is the setting, and, of course, he would return to earth as a setting, albeit a changed earth, in other novels. But his third novel, *Misson of Gravity* (1954), and a later sequel, *Star Light* (1971), which develops further the character of the aliens in the first as well as a related planetary environment, are masterworks of hard science fiction and of Clement's particular literary effects that are gullible only in their stubborn adherence to his values of accumulative knowledge and the ironic acceptance of the conditions of limitation inherent in partial and accumulating knowledge.

Mission of Gravity and *Star Light*, the two Mesklinite novels, are essentially stories of planet exploration on a grand scale although it is clear in both cases (as in other fictions that will be discussed later) that one, unique planet is being explored within a wide universe of variable possibilities. Both novels also are stories of communication because much of the exploration is done by non-human aliens working with human explorers and explorers from other species as well. In many cases, the goals and purposes of the various intelligent life forms do not coincide. Hence communication is often devious, indirect, and partial. But the sum total of the shrewdness, deviousness, and indirection of all species involved is always more knowledge for everyone. The knowledge is often new knowledge about the alien life forms themselves. The intelligent natives of Mesklin in *Mission of Gravity* learn a lot about Earth and about humans, and they cleverly and often deviously manage to acquire considerable human scientific knowledge in both novels. Clement's one concession here to narrative necessity is that the aliens all manage somehow to learn English and the humans to learn their languages, and this is a Herculean feat of language complexity given some of the variability of the physical forms involved. Further, the question of how much knowledge must be acquired by indirection or devious means is a major issue raised by Clement in both novels as the Mesklinites in particular manage to learn human science and technology. The reader, of course, also learns an immense amount of fictional, yet scientifically plausible, details about possible planetary environments in which conditions are widely variable.

GRAVITY AND WEATHER

On the solid principle that all life is part and parcel of the environment in which it evolves and lives, Clement has said that he began thinking about the setting for *Mission of Gravity* before he developed the now famous little aliens that inhabit it. An accepted notion in planet studies was that wide variations in gravitational force would not exist nearby in the same environment (apparently before Black Hole speculation), so Clement calculated the possible conditions that would allow an exception to this notion of non-variable gravity. In fact, he worked out the details of the planet Mesklin to the extent that with the serialization of the novel, and then in most subsequent publications of it, he included a nonfiction essay, "Whirligig World." This essay is mostly about the physical characteristics of the planet although the rhetoric of building a fiction out of astronomical and chemical analysis also pervades the essay. Clement challenges the reader to go through the analyses with him and to catch him in omissions or errors of calculation. Later, he admits that he was wrong in some details—but that is just part of the game in the detective, ironic puzzling he likes to do:

> I was a little unhappy when the MIT science fiction people [New England Science Fiction Association] buckled down and analyzed Mesklin and found that I was wrong, that it would actually have come to a sharp edge at the equator. On the other hand, if they were interested enough to steal computer time from the University and check up on this point, I suppose the story in a way was still fulfilling its aim of creating some fun. [41]

The fun that he was creating was also the serious matter of gradually trying out and accumulating new knowledge and doing this by dealing with variables—in this case variable gravity.

The notion of variability and of the possibility of error in a varied universe is such a key notion in all of Clement's work that an early use he makes of the word "variability," along with the usual literary effect of puzzling out a less than clearly revealed problem, would be helpful to see at this point. Also, the variability has to do with weather, which is a major image in both *Mission of Gravity* and *Star Light*. The story "Cold Front" (1946) was one creative result of his Air Force duty overseas because he said he thought of the idea for the story during the time he was doing meteorological work and flying while stationed in England. Humans trying to communicate and to trade with aliens of a planet called Hekla run into widely varying weather conditions that they have never encountered before because the planet is in a system with a star type that occasionally drops its luminosity when cirrus clouds of carbon particles form in its outer atmosphere. When the human scientists finally discover their ignorance of this fact, the peculiar Heklans (another minor example of fascinating aliens adapted to an unusual environment) have toyed with them to the point that the human weather expert nearly destroys his aircraft in an unexpected cold front:

> "If clouds are possible in a star's atmosphere, I'd say you had something on R Coronae quite similar to this cold front of yours right below us," he said. "If it happens very often, I suppose it's the explanation of the star's variability." [42]

Hekla's weather is more closely connected than ours with stellar changes, or rather the stellar variability is greater; and the Heklans are able to use this fact, by not telling all, to gain a certain power of knowlege over the human meteorologist. Similar elements, including variability in weather and in gravity as well as the competition for more and more knowledge, are key components of Clement's longer fictions about Mesklin and Mesklinites.

Mesklin, the planet itself, is a fascinating character in its own right as it is first presented in *Mission of Gravity*, discussed scientifically in "Whirligig World," used as a point of reference in *Star Light*, and returned to most recently in a 1973 short story, "Lecture Demonstration," which was written for a John Campbell memorial collection. Clement began speculating about the fictional planet in response to an astronomical puzzle that recent theorists now suggest can be solved by positing a black hole. In the double star system 61 Cygni, according to a paper published in 1943, the fainter star was observed to move around an invisible center of gravity sixteen times the mass of Jupiter that moved in turn around 61 Cygni A, a star somewhat smaller and dimmer than our sun. Clement speculated that the large invisible object in this system, which is not many light years from Earth, was a massive planet. He then set to work with analysis and slide rule to extrapolate the details of the system and, in particular, to construct a planet not just with high gravity, which was a familiar convention in science fiction, but with variable gravity. Reasoning that since Einstein suggested (and our astronauts train on the principle) "gravitational effects cannot be distinguished from inertial ones [and] the so-called centrifugal force is an inertial effect," Clement felt he could set his planet spinning rapidly enough to make his characters feel progressively lighter the closer they got to the equator. [43] Nevertheless, with its immense mass, the planet Mesklin exerts three times Earth gravity at the equator and nearly 700 Earth gravities at each pole.

Clement calls Mesklin "a rather weird-looking object" in his non-fiction discussion of the planet. The diameter at the equator is 48,000 miles, and from pole to pole along the axis it measures only 19,740 miles. The rate of spin for this massive object with the appearance of a fried egg is so rapid that a "day" on Mesklin is only seventeen-and-three-quarter minutes long. The seasons are also unusual on Mesklin as they are determined by the course of its elliptical orbit around its primary, which is a fairly dim red dwarf to start with, and by the tilt of its axis. Clement extrapolated a steep axial tilt and then combined this with a highly elliptical orbit that put the northern hemisphere in midsummer during the close short pass around its sun and left the same hemisphere with no sunlight for fully three quarters of the year. Thus the southern hemisphere of Mesklin with its long spring and summer faced toward the sun (twenty-eight months long as compared to two Earth months at the close end of the orbit) is farthest from the source of heat at its midsummer. The result is that nearly the entire northern hemisphere is an icecap of frozen methane during the majority of the year on Mesklin. The southern hemisphere contains oceans of liquid methane, and during the short two month pass near its sun, tremendous storms are generated across the equator as the polar icecap boils off and the seas rise. The storms are driven by methane vapor added to the atmosphere of nearly pure hydrogen under high pressure (large planets hold only their original hydrogen). Clement has carefully balanced temperatures, which are all very cold from our point of view since we know methane only as natural gas, with compounds that change at those temperatures to produce both dramatic weather conditions as well as a liquid and atmospheric base for the development of life.

The physical characteristics of the planet itself are not only a great intellectual game and scientific puzzle for Clement to work out, but also a source of irony and comic effect from the reader's anthropocentric and even heliocentric point of view. Winter for the Mesklinites becomes warmer, but not warm enough to boil away the methane in their bodies as long as they stay in the shielded southern hemisphere. Summer then becomes pleasantly cold (-165 degrees C) for the inhabitants of the southern half of the planet as Mesklin moves far from its sun. In other words, a long cold summer is proper weather for Mesklinites. Similarly, time duration on the rapidly spinning planet takes some getting used to for the few humans that do visit—only at the three-gravity equator. Occasionally Clement deliberately reverses the time terminology to emphasize this comic disparity. A human character will say to hurry, "We'll be out of here in a couple of hours!" The narrator adds, "Actually, it took less than three days (56 minutes)." [44] Mesklin is a very strange and fascinating world, indeed; but perhaps the most significant notion as Clement works out the details in this alien environment is again his sense of contingency, limitation, and variability. He knows that he cannot ever tell it all. "Whirligig World" says explicitly several places that there will always be more data to check. But like the shrewd little traders and explorers that inhabit Mesklin, Clement always seems to want to learn more, to speculate further.

LITTLE EPIC CHARACTERS AND JOURNEYS

If the planet Mesklin is peculiar from the point of view of Earth, the inhabitants are even stranger from the anthropocentric point of view. With a little of the tone of Swift, perhaps, they appear as Lilliputians on a Brobdingnagian world. But Clement is interested also in the plausible physical bases for life on Mesklin although he says in his nonfiction discussion of the planet that he feels no necessity to develop an explanation of all the inner life systems since even Earth biology has not yet achieved such comprehensiveness. The particular species of intelligent Mesklinites that shares the action with the human explorers in the two novels and the short story is a hydrogen-based life form. They require no lungs since the high pressure hydrogen is forced directly into their tissues.

23

They have multiple heart pumps working against the force of gravity. Liquid methane provides a workable body fluid, and vital energy comes apparently from reducing hydrocarbons rather than oxidizing them as with Earth life. With no lungs, Mesklinites produce a loud "hooting" sound from a siphon, and the langauge of the species we get to know in the fictions is called Stennish although only English is spoken at the time of the first novel. Mesklinites are fifteen inches in length, two inches in diameter, resemble caterpillars (though they have evolved an extremely touch chitinous exoskeleton under the immense gravity), and possess strong "nippers" for hands.

When *Missions of Gravity* opens, a human explorer, Charles Lackland, has been near the equator several Earth months. He has met a group of Mesklinites and taught their leader, Barlennan, enough English so that the two species can begin to learn from each other. Barlennan is a trader and captain of the sailing ship the *Bree*, which is constructed of what look like rafts lashed together and all built, like the natives, very close to the surface under the grip of Mesklinite gravity. The *Bree* is capable, however, of navigating tens of thousands of miles across the oceans of Mesklin's southern hemisphere. The home of Barlennan's people is near the south pole. Thus for Lackland to find them at such great distance and under the disorienting influence of what is for them light gravity indicates immediately the extent of their adventuresomeness and bravery. They refer to the equatorial region as "the rim" because one effect of high gravity on the atmosphere of Mesklin is to make the horizon appear higher than the viewer. Thus all Mesklinite maps are in the shape of bowls rather than globes. The greatest fear for a Mesklinite is to *fall* or to be *under* an object (the buildings that they prefer on Dhrawn in *Star Light* have transparent roofs) because the conditions of their evolution preclude entirely any activities such as jumping or throwing as we know them, and any fall at 600 Earth gravities would be immediately fatal.

Clement tells each of the Mesklinite stories in the omniscient third person, and at least half of the time his point-of-view character is either Barlennan or another of the Mesklinites in Barlennan's group. In other words, the reader is often told how incredible it is to conceive of a planet that would spin so slowly that one full rotation would take some eighty "days." The overall effect, of course, is that the reader learns a lot about the Mesklinite aliens from their points of view. At first they seem more suspicious, shrewd, and manipulative than humans. They work to conceal their true intentions on the assumption that the humans play the same game. As the Mesklinite stories go on, Clement does develop more duplicity in the human behavior so that Barlennan's manipulative strategies can be seen as proper analogues for human deception. In this sense, the alien point of view is a classic commentary on human vice and folly much in the manner that 18th-century satirists, such as Swift, used imaginary voyages. But Barlennan's motivations and behaviors are also truly alien and "Mesklinite" in a way that emphasizes one of Clement's major themes—the gradual accumulation of partial knowledge.

Three Mesklinite facts that affect their culture are important. Barlennan's people are traders in a very competitive environment. Mesklin is teeming with life forms (ironic in itself with such a low temperature liquid methane base), and the reader meets other intelligent, and not so intelligent, Mesklinite peoples all competing to outdo Barlennan's people. The second fact is that the normal Mesklinite life span, at least for Barlennan's people, is considerably longer than the human life span. In *Star Light*, we encounter an unbelieving and conde-

24

scending attitude of Barlennan's toward the humans who come and go so rapidly as he endures. Paradoxically, the third fact is implied by a physical characteristic of the planet Mesklin and mentioned briefly by Clement in his nonfiction account of the planet. Mesklin's steep axial inclination will cause a relatively rapid precession. In other words, the tilt of the planet reverses itself at frequent intervals (in millenial terms) so that life forms must establish themselves first on one hemisphere and then on the other. Hence pressures for evolutionary development must be similar to, but more rapid than, those produced by our Ice Ages. Barlennan and his people are ideal candidates to learn modern science and, especially, the technology of flight and space travel. They want to learn about new modes of travel and communications because it will give them trading advantages. They live long enough so that knowledge can accumulate in individuals, as well as in retrieval systems, and not have to be retaught often. Finally, an apparent long tradition of rapid evolutionary response to challenge provides the credible foundation for their obsession to learn.

Not only does Barlennan have a lot to learn about human science and technology, but also he must overcome his native fear of falling if he is ever to fly. The critic, Neil Barron, argues that these enormous obstacles that Barlennan's people must overcome, along with Clement's narrative structure of beginning the first fiction after the events of Barlennan's education have already commenced, make *Mission of Gravity* read like an epic. [45] Following the initial contacts between Lackland and Barlennan, the humans persuade the Mesklinites to undertake the incredibly long journey across land and sea to the south polar region to help them retrieve a valuable research rocket that is grounded in the high gravity. In shrewd Odysseus fashion, Barlennan agrees but hides his real motive from his human friends. Clement seems continually to ponder Barlennan's shrewd deception as the journey progresses. At the end of chapter twelve, Barlennan has the following conversation with his mate, Dondragmer:

> "I think you know by now what I'm really hoping to get out of this trip; I want to learn everything I possibly can of the Flyers' science. That's why I want to get to that rocket of theirs near the Center; Charles himself said that it contained much of the most advanced scientific equipment they have. When we have that, there won't be a pirate afloat or ashore who'll be able to touch the *Bree* . . . . That's why I wonder whether they'll tell what you want [Dondragmer is radioing up a question to the humans located now on one of Mesklin's moons]; they may suspect what I'm after."
>
> "I think you're too suspicious yourself. Have you ever *asked* for any of this scientific information you want to steal?"
>
> "Yes; Charles always said it was too difficult to explain."

In *Mission of Gravity*, the grave double issue of how much to tell and how much can be known is resolved suggestively as the epic journey of the little Mesklinites moves to its conclusion. When Barlennan and his crew finally locate the downed research rocket after many exotic and challenging adventures, the captain holds his discovery hostage. The humans are surprised. They had simply underestimated the drive for knowledge when life is long and matters are of great weight, or seen the other way, the Mesklinites are a small exaggeration of human drive and wiliness. In any case, Clement admires Mesklinites' stubbornness, and Barlennan's determination to forge ahead is not only resolution but also a bit of larceny. The humans agree to supply the Mesklinites with all the knowlege and technology that they are able to master. Lackland does point out, however, the limitation even in this program when he tells Barlennan that though "[he has] grown up from childhood surrounded by and even using those forces [electrical and nuclear energy] I do not understand them." Nevertheless, Barlennan wants to forge ahead. He replies, "We want to start *at the beginning*, knowing fully that we cannot learn all you know in our lifetimes."

SEQUELS, BELIEF, AND LIMITATIONS

The first journey of the Mesklinites ends with the image of the *Bree*, converted to a hot air balloon, rising to flight against the sublime polar gravity of Mesklin. In the two sequels written since that first journey, Clement gives a vignette from the College of Mesklin and describes another shrewd planet exploration. His short story, "Lecture Demonstration," is set back at the equatorial region of Mesklin where a human teacher and his Mesklinite students encounter a life and death geologic and chemical puzzle. His novel sequel, *Star Light*, which followed the usual pattern of initial serialization in *Analog* (the new name for *Astounding*) is the more ambitious use of Mesklinites and Mesklinite values for the exploration of another high gravity planet.

In the novel-length sequel, a task force of two-thousand presumed products of the College of Mesklin under the leadership of Barlennan have been eqipped with a small fleet of land-cruisers that seem to be a vehicular equivalent of the thin, flexible Mesklinite body used to explore a puzzling Type-Three planet that Clement names Dhrawn. Type-Three planets are large Jovian-like bodies that are very dense and for some reason have lost their hydrogen atmosphere. The question is whether this particular object ought to be labeled a star or planet since it emits more radiation than it receives from its dim primary, Lalande 21185. Dhrawn's rotational period is roughly two Earth months, and its atmosphere is a dynamic mix of oxygen, ammonia and water vapor at the proper temperatures to provide a confusing combination of freezing and thawing depending on the amounts of ammonia and water present. In any case, no human can explore Dhrawn because of the high gravity, and it is nearly as dangerous for Mesklinites because of the absence of high pressure hydrogen in the atmosphere. The place is also alien to the Mesklinites because of the "day" that is two Earth months long—or a little over 5000 of their "days." Nevertheless, Barlennan has agreed to take his group of explorers to the surface of Dhrawn under the direction and assistance of a small team of humans located in a control satellite six-million miles off the surface.

The reader can learn a good bit about Dhrawn, a body sublimely large like Mesklin but at the same time uniquely different from Mesklin, although Clement does not provide a nonfiction account of this planet-star. In fact, among the numerous unique planets and star systems that Clement explores fictionally, yet always plausibly, Mesklin is the only one that he has described in a nonfiction piece. He does describe settings among unusual star systems at times and then never writes a fiction at that location. But a good portion of the pleasure and excitement in Clement is to uncover the physical conditions around the variable universe as they appear in his fictions. The other puzzle that the reader is intrigued by in *Star Light*, of course, is what new knowledge the Mesklinites want to wrest from the humans and how they will do it. The action, then, in this sequel is one of exploration, clever deception, and the eventual broadening of the Mesklinite horizons. Not unexpectedly, perhaps, Barlennan's sailors have learned rocket flight by the end of *Star Light*.

Both Neil Barron and Clement himself have expressed some dissatisfaction with this later Mesklinite novel because it is too heavy with "technical exposition." [46] But what is most technical on Dhrawn is the unpredictability and variability of weather, and this, I think, is such a key image in Clement's work that the quintessence of the image seen working on Dhrawn makes the novel important. One of the major tasks for the Mesklinites is to gather weather data because, unlike the situation on Mesklin where the human observers could radio down more accurate forecasts from their closer satellites, the human weathermen are so distant from the surface of Dhrawn and so unfamiliar with the dynamic conditions that the puzzles are as immense as the globe of Dhrawn itself. Weather resulting from water, ammonia, and a source of internal radiation is a perfect symbol for variability. Near the beginning of chapter twelve, one of the human weather experts radios down to Dondragmer, who is commanding a land-cruiser frozen into some unknown ice: "There are just too many variables; with only water they are practically infinite . . . with water and ammonia together the number is infinitely squared."

The interaction among humans who are stationed on the control satellite and who plan the overall exploration is also greatly increased by Clement in this later Mesklinite novel. Also, other alien yet scientific species are with them as they agonize over what the Mesklinites are accomplishing for the expedition, and for themselves, on the surface of Dhrawn. (At the beginning of the next chapter, I will discuss the hints scattered by Clement through various novels of a fairly intricate community of intelligent species within five parsecs of Earth.) Perhaps the most interesting and well developed human character in *Star Light* is the linguist and diplomat, Elise Rich Hoffman (called Easy), who began to learn the Mesklinite language ten years before when her husband, Ib Hoffman, first was assigned as a planner to the Dhrawn project.

Star Light takes place fifty Earth years after *Mission of Gravity*. Easy is fluent in Stennish, and she and her husband have come a long way toward understanding Mesklinite character and appreciating their progressive deceptions. Their son, Benj, is a teenage apprentice on the project who develops a close attachment to a "young" Mesklinite, Beetchermarlf, as they practice language together over the radio. Beetch, who is a pilot of one of the land cruisers, eventually becomes the first Mesklinite space pilot. The significant point here, I think, in addition to the emphasis on language and diplomacy through the Hoffmans is Clement's focus on juvenile characters—even more so than in the Hunter fictions, in which the alien is much older than Bob.

In a sense, Barlennan and Dondragmer always seem young as they are encountered in both these novels. This is consistent with the belief that permeates each of the Mesklinite fictions. It is a belief in forging ahead, moving forward against great fears and obstacles, in a way that seems epic and yet refreshingly young at the same time. Early in the second novel, chapter five, Dondragmer expresses his philosophy, which is similar to Barlennan's as expressed in the last exchange with Charles Lackland. Both are straightforward, simple, even juvenile, and yet grounded in a wise and empirical sense of limitation. Similarly, the most representative humans in *Star Light* (the young ones, either in years or in spirit) share Dondragmer's belief: "Basically, his philosophy was the one he had just expressed: to do all one could in the time available, with the full knowledge that time would run out some day."

The Mesklinite fictions are Clement's most inspiring works. The images of variability and partial knowledge are open corridors to exploration and accumulating knowledge. The sense of immense fear and strangeness resolutely overcome is also inspiring. It is almost as though some powers of the Enlightenment oversee all the adventures of the Mesklinites, and small-minded pride is not part of their makeup—nor of ours as we watch them work. The Mesklinites know they are tiny, and they know that all knowledge is partial. Fortunately, Clement has provided them with long lives to accomplish their long journeys. A greater limitation than excessive technical jargon in Clement's work, though, is that with all their completeness as little heroic characters, the Mesklinites reveal to the reader no sense of generation—except for their longevity. Clement's Enlightenment fantasies include no attempts to portray either the technology of ill health (medicine) or the science of generation (sexuality), both of which are important and vital portrayals for realistic fiction. Beyond those omissions, however, the concerns in the Mesklinite fictions are important concerns that make Clement's universe seem to be an especially epic and full universe.

IV.

TENEBRA AND ABYORMEN: ABUNDANT LIFE

Whereas the resolute exploration journeys of the unlikely Mesklinites are key actions that make the Mesklinite novels meaningful and even epic, rich lyric description and celebration of the varieties of life and environment characterize two Clement novels about fictional worlds, *Close to Critical* and *Cycle of Fire*, that appeared between *Mission of Gravity* and *Star Light*. Together these four "planet novels" people a section of the universe within relative close proximity to our Solar System, and they achieve an imaginative depth of image and suggestion about plenitude and variety in life that may be Clement's finest contribution to our culture. When we look at the night sky within five parsecs of Earth, we see a variety of stellar phenomena and much emptiness. When we read Clement's fictions about Mesklin and Dhrawn, Tenebra, Abyormen, and their systems, we are fascinated by alien life forms in such abundance, variety, and plausible consistency (except for the fact that life beyond this planet is still only an hypothesis) that these imaginative speculations may take precedence over any other literary effects. At least the abundance and variety are major factors in the overall literary effect of this portion of Clement's work. Shorter fictions, also, as we shall see later fill in smaller pieces here and there of his baroque puzzle of alien life within the nearby universe.

Clement is too much a believer in probabilities and the limitations of perception, however, to construct a fully developed imaginative universe. His is no system of worlds as complete as we find in the work of Frank Herbert nor as inter-related even as the peopled Galaxy of Isaac Asimov's *Foundation Trilogy*. Furthermore, unlike other universe makers in the space opera of science fiction who dwell on war or politics among worlds, Clement imagines one related set of motivations that governs all his alien life from the small Mesklinites to the large Drommians, who resemble otters, to the nitrogen life Observers in his latest novel. He does differentiate some character traits, such as the super shrewdness of Mesklinites, and he hints at others that he may develop later, such as paranoia among Drommians. But essentially all life in Clement is curious and eager to learn about other life, and the learning processes are always complex, sometimes devious. In fact, the clever ploy that Barlennan uses in *Star Light* to help him wrest the knowledge of space flight from his human teachers is a fiction he invents about alien life on Dhrawn. In other words, Clement's fictions about alien life forms, in themselves, may be seen as clever ploys to wrest more knowledge, more speculation, out of the reader. Dhrawn, the giant ball of rock that may be a partial star object, apparently contains no native life form, but the novel, *Star Light*, contains Clement's most developed hints about other life forms within five parsecs of Earth. Just as Barlennan uses fiction as a clever lie to get at the truth, so Clement's novel suggests links among several of his other fictions into one living universe.

The catalog of alien life that he presents is built from his previous work and, also, certainly lays the speculative groundwork for future fictions he may never get around to writing. In the passages from *Star Light*, Clement refuses to speculate about any over-riding plan or "divine design" that would link his various worlds. He is too skeptical for that. He does place each of them in a time continuum, however, of scientific development and energy utilization that is very earth centered. In other words, his alien life forms are an ironic mix of the totally alien and the anthropocentric seeker after knowledge. Hints appear throughout *Star Light*, but Ib Hoffman gives the most concise statement of the catalog that links Mesklin to Tenebra and beyond:

> You know as well as I do that in the very small volume of space within five parsecs of Sol, with only seventy-four known stars and about two hundred sunless planets, what we have found in the way of intelligence: twenty races at about our own stage of development, safely past their Energy Crisis; eight, including Tenebra and Mesklin, which haven't met it yet; eight which failed to pass it and are extinct; three which failed but have some hope of recovery; every one of them, remember, within a hundred thousand years of that key point in their history, one way or the other! That's in spite of the fact that the planets range in age from Panesh's nine billion years or so to Tenebra's maybe a tenth of that. [47]

Hoffman refuses to be mystical, but there does seem to be a plenitude of intelligence all moving along the same path in Clement's worlds. Nevertheless, like all skeptical empiricists, Clement seems more interested in concrete particulars (out of which the reader can discover patterns of images) than in speculative unities.

CLOSE TO CRITICAL (1964)

Close to Critical was serialized in *Astounding Science Fiction* in 1958 although it did not appear in book form until 1964. In other words, except for Dhrawn, Clement had completed all his major fictional world building by the end of the Fifties, and in chronological order the conception of the planet Abyormen and its peculiar system in the novel *Cycle of Fire* (1957) preceded the conception and development of this fiction about the planet Tenebra. In order of creation, Clement first developed the planet Mesklin with a storyline of human exploration of the planet that was actually done by aliens cooperating more or less with the humans. Later, he returned to this same storyline of human cooperating with alien to explore two other exotic planets, Tenebra in this novel and Dhrawn in the Mesklinite sequel, *Star Light*. In between, Clement presents the planet Abyormen by means of a different narrative pattern, which is perhaps more effective as a dramatic action and which also includes some of his most powerful imagery. But his repeated narrative pattern of presenting human explorers hovering in orbit above giant planet bodies as they work, and in some cases are worked by alien agents who are at home in the alien environments, is not an ineffective storyline. Furthermore, the links of consistency and difference that tie together the several projects of exploration may be important in Clement's partially complete universe of partial knowledge.

The project to explore Tenebra in *Close to Critical* is midway in time between the Mesklin exploration and the Dhrawn project. Easy Hoffman, who is the important linguist, diplomat, and mother of the teenager Benj in the Dhrawn project, was first created by Clement as the twelve-year-old Easy Rich in this novel. The reader sees her for the first time showing a young Drommian around the control satellite for the Tenebran project. The project itself is the familiar and intricately engineered set of scientific experiments intended to gather data about a very non-Earthlike planet. The project had begun some 16 years before the time of the novel, that is before Easy Rich was born and apparently about the time of the founding of the College of Mesklin, when the human explorers had landed an incredibly constructed robot on the surface of Tenebra. The success of this robot, patiently controlled from the satellite during the intervening sixteen years, sets the scene for the story involving Easy, the young Drommian, and two groups of alien Tenebrites.

In Clement's usual and effective manner, the conditions on Tenebra both determine the story and provide some of the most interesting revelations of the novel. The planet belongs to the well-known star, Altair, brightest star in the Constellation Aquila, about sixteen light years from Earth in the general direction of the Constellation Cygnus—or relatively close to Mesklin. Clement's explorers fan out in that interesting portion of our galaxy as he tells us in *Star Light*. Although Altair is a first magnitude white star, ten times the brightness of our sun, Tenebra is almost devoid of visible light for humans on its surface (hence the name for the planet) because of an extremely dense atmosphere. The atmospheric gases are heavy, water vapor and a fair amount of free oxygen; and with the size of the planet, three Earth diamters, plus its mass, atmospheric pressure on Tenebra equals nearly 800 times that of Earth. Under such high pressure and with sufficient radiation from Altair, the temperature on Tenebra is near the critical temperature of water. A Tenebran "day" is about four Earth days, and each night the temperature drops just enough to turn the lower atmosphere into liquid water. During the day on Tenebra, however, temperatures rise above water's critical temperature at that atmospheric pressure so that only water vapor is possible. All the rivers and ponds evaporate. Large bodies of oily sludge and other liquids, such as sulphuric acid, however, do remain from day to day.

Once again Clement has imagined physical conditions that not only are interesting and plausible in their own right as intellectual puzzles but also mirror the details of his story about flight. Further, the physical conditions suggest thematic ideas that make his stories meaningful. Easy and her Drommian companion nearly die, come close to "critical," under the hostile conditions of high temperature, high pressure, and high gravity. But perhaps even more interesting than the plot complications, which will be described below, is the notion of "critical" flux. The continual daily movement on Tenebra back and forth around the critical temperature of water at this enormous pressure (about 370 degrees fahrenheit according to Clement's calculations) produces a sense of flux and "weather" entirely different from any planet, real or fictional, that we are familiar with, one that is changeable and variable. In this case, weather is not wind and convection currents (the pressure is too high) but rather the continuous diurnal change from liquid to gas and back again under a heavy gravitational pull. The following passage, spoken by one of the humans to the Drommian father of Easy's companion from near the end of chapter three, communicates well this image of flux, which is so different from Mesklin or Hekla and is a key image in all of Clement's varieties of weather:

> Tenebra is a rather strange planet, Diastrophism is like Earth's weather; the question is not whether it will rain tomorrow but whether your pasture will start to grow into a hill . . . . The general cause we know—the atmosphere is mostly water near its critical temperature, and silicate rocks dissolve fairly rapidly under those circumstances. The place cools off just enough each night to let a little of the atmosphere turn liquid, so for the best part of two Earth days you have the crust washing down to the oceans like the Big Rock Candy Mountain. With three Earth gravities trying to make themselves felt, it's hardly surprising that the crust is readjusting all the time.

The explorers orbiting the planet actually dispute whether these daily changes of the atmosphere from gas to liquid should be called "weather" since in the tight envelope of Tenebra's atmosphere there are normally no convection currents and hence no wind. In fact, the discussions of the reasons for the absence of wind sound like the early meteorologists of the 18th century, such as Erasmus Darwin. In the development of the scientific action of the story, "wind" finally does appear, at a two m.p.h. hurricane rate for Tenebra, when an active volcano forces convection currents into the atmosphere. But regardless of weather terminology, the "pressure cooker" conditions on Tenebra certainly manifest themselves in results that suggest dynamic flux. Similarly, the action of the characters in the novel demonstrates an interesting sense of flux, and in this instance in Clement's work, the conflicts grow out of the tensions of adolescence and, even, generation. I think finally that the writing about character and personality tension is not as successful in this novel as Clement's excitement about environment even though the environmental vividness, as usual in Clement, provides analogues for inner tension. But Clement does conceive several provocative relationships here among aliens and humans and between creatures and a machine.

The robot lander that has been on the surface of Tenebra since the project began not only is engineered to withstand the pressure and corrosive effect of what Clement nicely terms the "ambiguous" atmosphere but also is a clever and efficient communications device that allows the human explorers to establish a remarkable remote control. The robot is named Fagin, and like Dickens's leader of orphan children in *Oliver Twist*, the machine (as the voice and body of the remote humans, of course) succeeds partially in training young natives nearly to be criminals to their traditions. [48] Among a myriad of lesser biological types that Clement always builds consistently into his worlds, the most intelligent life form on Tenebra is an egg-laying, cone-shaped species with scales, spiny crests that serve as organs of vision capable of fair sight in Tenebran darkness, and body fluids with some part sulphuric acid that indicates an evolution like Earth vertebrates out of their part sulphuric acid oceans. These Tenebrites have language and analytic minds since for Clement intelligence across the universe is defined by the ability to analyze and the desire to know, but they are at the lower stages of cultural and technological development.

After a period of time exploring the surface, Fagin cleverly steals some fresh eggs from a nest area of this caveman species and during the years preceding the main action of the novel nurtures his own village of more advanced Tenebrites. This group of agents for human exploration of the planet is taught to make fire from Tenebran wood, a skill that permits them a mobility at night that the natives have never had since the agents can evaporate the descending atmosphere. But most importantly the Tenebrites are taught English and thus the potential for an Earth science-based technology. Ironically, the most advanced art that Fagin teaches these aliens in the novel is the construction of rudimentary rafts to allow them to venture for the first time onto their planet's changing oceans whereas the Mesklinites, under entirely different conditions, were skillful sailors when the human teachers arrived.

Fagin as "teacher," then, manages a group of Tenebrite adolescents who adapt so well to scientific method that toward the end of the novel they consider momentarily taking their teacher apart to see what makes him work. The orphaned and eager young Tenebrites are approximately the same age as twelve-year-old Easy Rich and her Drommian companion, who is the youngest of the group in developmental age. Clement now and then has the Drommian act childish to provide a tension that seems to be the weakest part of the novel. The plot of the novel is determined when Easy and the Drommian accidentally descend to the surface in an unfinished research bathyscaphe. They can survive in the bathyscaphe but are unable to return to orbit. Fagin's students are sent to locate the ship with the plan that they can be directed in the completion of some outside circuitry that will solve the problem. Actually, a tribe of naive, though apparently warlike, Tenebrites gets to the ship ahead of Fagin's students and solves the problem in a more native and organic manner. They inject the bathyschaphe tanks with hydrogen from an indigenous life form that, in conjunction with the convection from the nearby volcano, allows it to rise. Thus, human science is augmented by native wit—not exactly outsmarted as in the Mesklinite novels but added to—and the overall effect is the sense of cooperative intelligence.

Two intelligence traits or skills seem central to this story, as in so much of Clement's work, and in part these traits and skills are particularly native to the dynamic flux of adolescence that is represented by Easy, by the Tenebrites as a primitive, young species as well as the particular Tenebrites that Fagin has stolen, and by the planet itself, perhaps, as a young planet in developmental flux. The first trait is the remarkable fluency with languages. Everyone is good with languages, but Easy is particularly gifted. In chapter nine, her father says, "She'll learn any language she can pronounce nearly as fast as you can give it to her, Doctor." The second trait is the familiar appeal to knowledge that we see everywhere in Clement's work. In chapter seven, Fagin delivers a long speech to the warlike Tenebrites that one of the young stolen and apparently turncoat Tenebrites has to translate (he's learned his native language as a second language). Strangely enough, the power of this positivistic rhetoric prevails against whatever the instinctual urges of these primitive natives of the dark planet might be. Fagin even hopes he might train the non-English speakers electrically:

> If you can find this machine in which my friends are caught, and learn from me how to fix it, they will be able to go back up once more and bring things for you all; if you can't or won't, my people will die here, and there will not even be knowledge for you—for some day I will die, too, you know.

Thus on Tenebra, the planet of shade, flux, and darkness, the Enlightenment of knowledge prevails. Even though there is the suggestion of giving beads to the Indians, Fagin's main selling point is knowledge. Clement's images and the sense of the strange environment itself are superb in this novel, and the tensions peculiar to adolescence are also consistent with these images. Clement knew what he wanted in the mix, but there is also a certain clumsiness in the narrative that may even be artistically determined to coincide with the notion of adolescence. At one point, an English-speaking Tenebrite says, "Fagin would have had something to say about that sentence." In other words, Clement is self-conscious about his use of language. But when he was asked about the name that he gave to the planet itself, Clement denied any intention to suggest the religious and liturgical notion of Tenebra and, in fact, said he would not have used the name if he had thought of that. [49]

CYCLE OF FIRE (1957)

If there may be a certain unfulfilled potential for meaningful symbolism in Tenebra, a profound suggestiveness about life and death coupled with a restatement of his belief in scientific methodology are fully realized in Clement's novel about a system in the Pleiades that contains his fictional planet Abyormen. Clement has said that Andre Lwoff's article entitled "The Life Cycle of a Virus," which appeared in the March 1954 *Scientific American*, gave him the idea for *Cycle of Fire*. Not only is the content of Lwoff's piece referred to in chapter fourteen of the novel but also the poetic tone of this scientific article underlies the novel. [50] Lwoff describes the way certain viruses are capable of remaining dormant inside the totally alien life form of certain bacteria for several generations before they reappear as distinct virus life, and he emphasizes the cycles of life and death coupled here with reproduction and the protection of generation. Although much of Clement's fiction avoids such sublime and poetic images, *Cycle of Fire* is meant to demonstrate, on this most elemental level of life and death (not microscopic in the novel, of course), the symbiotic inter-dependence of what seem to be very alien life forms.

He had written about symbiosis in *Needle* and its sequel, but here it is part of novels of world building and hence more alien, more sublime. Actually, the theme is completely central to Clement's work since each of the planet explorations described above are symbiotic in that close cooperation is essential to the success of each project. The theme is also consistent with and central to his overriding belief in the scientific methodology of accumulative knowledge or partial knowledge. No one explorer, investigator, or life form is self sufficient. Dependence and cooperation—even to the point of apparent ironies when far distant things become closely related, such as Tenebrites and Fagin—are essential to the survival, growth, and well being of what seem to be alien races. The strange relationship between the "cold life" and the "hot life" on Abyormen, as it is gradually revealed in the novel and as it is mirrored in the relationship between the young human explorer and his Abyormenite friend, is certainly one of Clement's most effective images for symbiosis.

Several unusual characteristics of the setting and of the narrative structure in this novel set it apart from the other planet novels that have been discussed immediately above. The planet Abyormen, its life forms, and the exploration itself are not really included in the little segment of our Galaxy within 5 parsecs of Earth that makes up the common environment of the Mesklinite novels and Tenebra. It is almost as though Clement intends to remove Abyormen far away from the common ground of exploration to pursue his profoundest images about life and death. In other words, the novel stands out as a bit unusual for this hard science-fiction writer who about the same time in his writing is carefully exploring the varieties of one strange world after another relatively nearby Earth. Whereas 5 parsec include an area no more distant approximately than seventeen light years from Earth, the planet Abyormen is in the Pleiades and part of a system with the brightest star in that cluster, Alcyone, which Clement says is some 500 light years from Earth.

Actually, Abyormen orbits a small red dwarf star named Theer by the natives and invisible to our telescopes. The friction of Theer and its planet may have caused the creation of the huge blue sun Alcyone, which the natives call Arren, out of the nebulosity of the Pleiades cluster; or Alcyone may have captured Theer. The result is a three-body system in which Abyormen and Theer orbit Alcyone, or Arren, in an extremely eccentric orbit that is both unstable and also produces the wide variations in temperature that have resulted in the evolution of the symbiotic cold life and hot life forms. Further, the instability of the system means it has a relatively imminent mortality which complements the other notions of mortality in the novel.

Not only does Clement set this novel farther from Earth than is usual for him then, but also the human exploration of the system seems to be taking place in fictional time much before the discovery and exploration of Mesklin and the subsequent planet projects. Perhaps in Clement's universe, what the human explorers and scientists are able to learn on Abyormen, far away and early in our history of space travel, about life and death and methodological cooperation is the necessary prerequisite for the later projects. The usual need in literature for deep philosophic meaning is often apparently ignored by a writer, such as Clement, as he works out what seem to be more empirically based puzzles. But in this novel there are hints of more Romantic concerns, plus deviations from Clement's usual practice, that seem to emphasize this kind of intention.

The narrative structure in which Clement chooses to place the story of this planet and the encounters with its alien inhabitants is also different. Rather than the remote control of alien agents from an orbiting satellite and radio communication with them as they journey across their planet, this novel involves the direct companionship between a human and an alien as they journey together. What is lost, of course, are the extreme varieties of planetary conditions that prevent humans from setting foot on the surface. What is gained is a closer human friendship with an alien. Except for its wildly eccentric orbits (Abyormen also orbits Theer unusually to allow Clement to include many more fascinating details of astronomy), this planet is relatively earthlike when it is in its cold-life part of the orbit around Alcyone. During the latter part of one of these "seasons," when the conditions are favorable to our kind of life, a young space cadet named Nils Kruger, "who has grown up on Earth during the first decade of interstellar exploration," is shipwrecked and apparently left for dead on Abyormen. He meets—actually saves the life of—an alien named Dar Lang Ahn, who has also just crashed his own glider and is trying to make his way home across the planet before the hot season comes on. The story then develops as a true picaresque journey adapted to science-fiction needs. It is not primarily an exploratory journey although much is learned. The reader watches a friendship grow between human and alien as they learn each other's language and support each other in the journey. Adventures are encountered and obstacles overcome. But the primary action is the gradual uncovering, not so much the physical conditions, but the nature of life and death on Abyormen.

Contrary to his usual practice in creating alien life, Clement seems to have given Dar a biochemistry much like Kruger's, and Dar is humanoid in appearance though only four-and-a-half feet tall with claws for digits. When Kruger meets him, Dar is carrying a heavy pack of books that must be gotten to his "teachers" in the north before the hot season arrives. As their friendship grows with their ability to communicate, Kruger gradually learns the details of the unusual life cycles on Abyormen. He learns more when they finally get to the teachers at the Ice Ramparts. Dar's species is the "cold life" complement of the planet, able to thrive on the surface for a period no more than 65 terrestrial years at a cycle. But taking into account the transitional time in the orbit as the planet changes from hot to cold, the life span for every member of Dar's species is 830 of their "years," that is orbits around Theer, with each year lasting about 18 terrestrial days. Thus Dar is a little over forty of Kruger's years when they meet, and in an uncanny way he knows the exact date of his coming death. During the hot season, a few members of Dar's species survive deep within the Ice Ramparts at the planet's ice cap and become the teachers whose job it is to preserve the culture and memories of the people until the next cold season.

As the story develops and the reader gets to know Dar and his cold-life species, the puzzle of how the symbiosis with the hot-life complementary species works is gradually unraveled. Hot-life teachers are not seen until the very end of the narrative, and in the meantime human explorers and scientists have returned to Abyormen and help Kruger unravel the mystery. Hot-life creatures are very different in appearance. For one thing, they don't have to be Kruger's companion and friend on the journey north; and so Clement can indulge his imaginaton for aliens. They are melon-shaped with six limbs and a radial, rather than a bilateral symmetry. They look to Kruger and his friends like "fat-bodied starfish." Along with Dar's books, which allow an eloquent celebration of the role of literature to accumulate and to pass on a little bit of knowledge here and there, Clement continually enriches the narrative with details about these complementary life forms. Gratuitous little scientific hints appear in all his writings. For example, in terms of vision the binary star system that holds Abyormen is bound to cause unusual and interesting varieties of enlightenment. Dar's eyes, set on the sides of his head, function independently of one another, and he sees farther into the infra-red portion of the spectrum than Kruger does. But during the hot season under the brutal rays of a closer Alcyone, vision would be impossible. the human scientists discover that the hot-life species "sees" by means of sound waves. Nevertheless, the more technologically advanced hot-life teachers have developed a rudimentary knowledge of the astronomy of their system. These two gratuitous asides—about books and about sightless astronomy—are examples of the rich details that Clement puzzles over in each of his alien worlds.

Kruger and then his human rescuers speculate at first that the cold-life and hot-life forms on Abyormen are complementary forms of the same species, like butterflies and caterpillars. But they are puzzled about how reproduction is accomplished and why the phases have to correspond exactly with the orbit around Alcyone. In fact, they see the life form in its two varieties as perhaps the most adaptable in the universe, which is frightening to them. It is only after a long conversation by television robot with a hot-life teacher who is protected deep inside a volcanic cavern that they deduce the true secret of the Abyormenite symbiosis. This is modeled, of course, after the virus/bacteria symbiosis in the Lwoff article. The scientists actually paraphrase parts of the article in chapter fourteen of the novel. Clement does leave the details fuzzy in this case, but as the ideas are translated to Abyormenite biology, two conclusions are drawn emphatically and poignantly. The species are not one but rather are alien to each other, and death is necessary for reproduction for both:

> The really important fact is that *Dar Lang Ahn's people have to die in order to reproduce* . . . . the "hot" and "cold" forms are completely alien types of life, which originally evolved independently. [then the virus paraphrase] . . . a similar ability has developed here—that every cell of a being like Dar Lang Ahn has in its nucleus the factors which will produce one of those starfish under the proper conditions.

The narrative conclusion to the novel expresses a human pathos in a direct way that is unusual for Clement. From the time of his rescue midway in the story, Kruger's plan had been to make Dar indispensable as a teacher so that he would not have to die at the completion of his appointed span of 830 Abyormenite years. The friendship had grown strong between the two, and this is a special symbiosis of alien to alien. But Dar's native instinct to reproduce by dying prevails. This is combined with a new understanding of scientific method that complements his earlier allegiance to his books—in this case, then, a symbiosis of methods. Kruger has actually taught Dar better than he had intended. He has taught him that partial knowledge accumulated gradually is the best method, and thus in a sense he has taught him a method of dying that goes along well with Abyormenite instincts. As Dar says goodbye to his human friend in the final scene of the novel, the reader should notice the several symbioses. The alien speaks like a fully emotional human. The humans will help the alien descendants of Dar overcome the instability of the Alcyone system in the future. Furthermore, all of this is in the context of scientific method which, since it builds syntheses out of unrelated pieces of data, may be seen as a symbiosis of parts that may be alien to each other. Here in Dar's final words to Kruger, also, is the fusion of scientific method to deep feeling, and this may be the most meaningful symbiosis of all in *Cycle of Fire*:

> I could have stayed down below [inside the Ice] and dictated scores of books about everything I had seen you do or heard you say, but even though I understood a good deal of it my people wouldn't. There was something else they needed more, and gradually I came to understand what it was.
>   It's *method*, Nils. It's the very way you people go about solving

36

problems—imagination and experiment together . . . . Of course, the facts are important too, but I didn't give too many of those. Just scattered pieces of information here and there, so that they could check their answers once in a while . . . . Nils, many of your years from now there will be quite a lot of my people who are part of me. I will be gone, but you may still be around. Maybe with what you and I have done for them some of those people will be scientists, and will have learned to get respect instead of contempt from the "hot" ones, and to start something which may in time be a civilization like yours. I would like to think that you will be helping them.

FINAL COMMENT ON ALIEN WORLD NOVELS

In his experimental and rather bitter recent novel about the limitations in science-fiction writing, *Galaxies*, Barry Malzberg laments that effective narratives about alien life are impossible and inadviseable and that the writer has left to him only to explore the depths of the self. He says bluntly, "It would be nice to compound the myth of faster-than-light drive with deeper and richer myths of strange races amidst the great stars, but this cannot be." [51] Hal Clement has admitted that one of his few concessions to scientific implausibility has been his assumption of some means of faster-than-light travel. Following that assumption, he has not hesitated to people the stars with strange races. The four novels discussed in these two chapters are his most elaborate contributions in this vein. The Mesklinites are his most provocative aliens. Tenebra, also, is an interesting place with interesting and different people. The deeper questions of life, death, and generation are not his usual environment, but the symbioses on Abyormen are effective and inform all his aliens from earth outward. Clement has certainly attempted what Malzberg says cannot be done.

V.

JUVENILES AND NOVELS OF EARTH

If thus far in Clement's work we have celebrated the varieties of life he imagines and the varieties of weather and other changing conditions that he weaves into his fictions, from now on in this study we will discuss in somewhat less depth the varieties of writing that fill out his career to date. The final chapter, then, will conclude with a brief summary of his overall effects. Although his most profound and successful fiction is contained in the Needle novels and the planet novels, Clement attempted a variety of writing in addition to those six most effective novels. Not only can a consistency of interests and thematic material be noticed throughout his lesser work but also a self-conscious concern with the craft and strategies of science fiction can be seen. In other words, Clement is not merely an imaginative scientist who mingles experiment and imagination as Dar Lang Ahn observes of all human extrapolators. He is also a literary artist struggling with various forms throughout a long and varied career that promises to continue for some time. This chapter will deal with two juvenile novels and two novels set on Earth. The next two chapters will deal briefly with the varieties of shorter forms he wrote, his most recent novel, and then summarize his overall effects and major themes or ideas.

Since the majority of the characters that have already been discussed in

Clement's six major novels and certainly all of the more interesting characters, both human and alien, have been blessed with the fresh, eager-to-learn traits of adolescents, it is not surprising that he should have marketed a book or two directly for the juvenile market. But Clement is especially self-conscious about the juvenile form (if it is a form distinct from all of the science fiction that traditionally has had a particular appeal for young people). He counts his one novel that was specifically presented as a juvenile as one of his most doubtful works:

> [The Ranger Boys in Space] was commissioned by the L. C. Page Company in the mid-fifties with the specific notion of reviving such things as the Motorcycle Boys and other series which had done so well so long, and I deliberately followed that general format. The day had passed, I fear; the book grossed me about $45, and I suspect you'd have a good deal of trouble getting hold of a copy anywhere. [52]

During this same period of prolific writing in the decade of the fifties, he also produced an historical novel for juveniles that remained unpublished for twenty years, Left of Africa (1976). The fact that Clement could not, or would not, adopt the juvenile form wholeheartedly, despite his tendency to make his favorite characters juveniles and to express values that are predominant in juvenile literature (values about technological ingenuity, invention, and adventure), is an indication of his totally serious artistic and even philosophic intentions for science fiction. [53] The juvenile form, in a way, has always been Clement's primary mode, but his artistic intentions have always been serious and organic as well.

TWO JUVENILES

Clement's two juvenile novels, The Ranger Boys in Space and Left of Africa, contain some very provocative images and ideas that link both of them closely to his other work, especially his planet novels. In the eleventh chapter of Cycle of Fire, right after Kruger's fellow spacemen have returned to Abyormen, Clement describes Dar Lang Ahn's first flight off the planet; the reaction of this new space traveler (not an adolescent, though) to zero gravity or free fall is commented on by the narrator:

> The only time he [Dar] looked down for more than a moment at a time was when circular velocity was reached and the tender went weightless. Then he looked back at the surface for nearly a minute and, to the sincere astonishment of all watchers, took the phenomenon in his stride. Apparently he had convinced himself that the falling sensation did not represent an actual fall or, if it did, that the pilots would take care of the situation before it became dangerous. Major Donabed developed a healthy respect for Dar Lang Ahn in that moment; he had experienced too many educated human beings who had become hysterical in like circumstances.

The theme of hysteria in the free fall of microgravity is central to The Ranger Boys in Space, and Clement's notions of how to cope with that sensation are important in understanding the overall effects in his work. In that respect, *The Ranger Boys in Space* has a very serious story to tell. Perhaps Clement's concern about weightlessness, which is inserted gratuitously into *Cycle of Fire* and that becomes the key idea in this juvenile novel written about the same time, is a product of the concerns of the decade of the fifties in America when very little was known experimentally about microgravity and there were real fears that it would present an obstacle to human space travel. Certainly the possibility of men being able to function in space is essential to Clement's imaginings. He faces the issues and fears squarely in *The Ranger Boys in Space*.

In the novel, adults are immobilized by the nausea and disorientation of weightlessness. The prime reason, according to Clement, is that the body, as it matures, adjusts itself totally to earth environment. The consequence will be that unless the body can somehow adapt to different environments there can be no space program. At the end of chapter two, Uncle Jim, who is the central adult for the Ranger boys, sums up the problem, and it is really the issue of anthropocentrism:

> What we're facing is the fact that man spends a lifetime training his mind and nervous system to link together the messages from his muscles, his eyes, and his semicircular canals [the inner ear]; now he faces a situation where those messages disagree with each other. It's no wonder his mind quits under the strain. I'm afraid, Pete, that we're not going to walk around on the deserts of Mars—ever.

Clement's "juvenile" solution that will save the space program and allow for the exploration of variety and non-anthropocentric difference throughout the universe is for young, orphaned boys to lead the way in learning to tolerate the sensations of disorientation in free fall. Although they are developed rather superficially in this book, the factors are profound: young and eager minds adapt to difference more easily; the orphaned state means that ties and obligations to the past are minimal; the factor of males as the better explorers makes less sense and, of course, is contradicted by Clement in his favorite character of the young girl Easy Rich as explorer. Nevertheless, Clement's model for our first astronauts is clearly presented in this juvenile novel in a way that seems particularly consistent with the rest of his work. For him, the "right stuff" must take acount of the unusual disorientation from parochial earthbound perspectives that space travel will present, and to adjust to this sense of difference, the astronaut must be young, unencumbered by attachments, and eager. [54] Finally, free fall itself is a profound image for the sense of limitation, or partial knowledge, that always accompanies these young people and that helps to leave their minds open to the continual acquisition of new knowledge. Again, it is Uncle Jim, midway in chapter seventeen, who reflects this universal condition of falling:

> . . . anything else that might serve to keep his mind from the frightful sensations he was enduring. The boys had said it was easy—all right, so he was falling; what difference did it make? So was the moon; so was the earth, and they never hit anything. His mind knew he was safe, but his body didn't believe it.

In spite of the importance of these images and ideas, there is a definite silliness to this narrative that is determined undoubtedly by Clement's adherence to the juvenile form. The title characters are named Bart and Dart Ranger (Dart is a quick 15-year-old to Bart's more mature 16), and together with a couple friends, they are even closer to Hardy Boy types than the gang in the two Needle novels. The space program itself in the book, which eventually lands the boys as the first humans on the Moon, has little of the mammoth technological and governmental complexity that we are used to in America. Indeed, except for the problem of weightlessness, Clement's juvenile patterns here allow him to take it all very casually. The one additional theme that energizes the writing, and is probably also part of the pattern, is the enthusiasm of the young people for the space program. The stereotypic stowaway kid who ends up making the greatest breakthrough (he is the first actually to reach the Moon almost by accident) says it best. His name is Tumble Tighe, and he's referred to as the "impatient pal" of the Ranger boys. When Tumble is discovered and confronted at the end of chapter eight, his enthusiastic rhetoric wins out: "I want to go more than you ever wanted to read a new book! I've wanted to see the moon and Mars and Venus since I knew what they were . . . . Bring on your rocket."

If one of the purposes of juvenile literature is to encourage adventures in reading, as Tumble's argument to one of the Ranger boy gang suggests, along with the adventuresome desire for new knowledge, Clement's overall interests (both literary and scientific) are ideally suited for the form. He does not like the non-serious association of writing only for juveniles, as I suggested at the start, because he is very serious about the meanings in his work. Probably since *The Ranger Boys in Space* did not turn out as a genuine *Tom Sawyer*, he went back to hard science fiction. But he did write one other explicitly juvenile book, at about the same time in the fifties, in which the sense of new discovery is expressed in a moving way and included in a narrative structure about discovery on Earth that is a fine complement to the planet novels. *Left of Africa* was actually discovered some 20 years after Clement wrote it by a fan who liked Clement's work so much that he published that book in 1976. The jacket advertisement for the novel reads in part:

> *Left of Africa* was written before *Cycle of Fire* and after *Mission of Gravity*. It is not science fiction. It is a juvenile historical adventure. But it has that same breath of pure reason that makes Hal Clement's science fiction great . . . . *Left of Africa* is about, among other things, a scientific discovery, one of the most basic scientific discoveries of all time.

The story takes place 2500 years ago and follows a bright, twelve-year-old boy, Gizona, on a series of adventures that take him eventually on a circular journey all the way around Africa, starting east from southern Spain and ending up back at Gibraltar. Not only is the structure of the narrative circular, ending at the location where it began, but also the main action is Gizona's gradual deduction that "the world is a ball." To survive, the boy has to be quick and clever like Barlennan, and he is also endowed by Clement with a near perfect memory. In other words, the story is about learning—about perception, deduction, language, epistemology. Clement takes the opportunity to develop all these topics as he follows Gizona through one adventure after another. Gizona is also a loner, an orphan, but the important thing is his tremendous desire and capability for working out new knowledge. The clever little hero deduces the Earth's roundness by noticing the sun moving to the north of the sky at noon and the familiar constellations disappearing and then reappearing as the loop around Africa is made. At the end, he suggests that they sail to the "left" of Africa (a curious map-orientation way of seeing for Clement) to see if the world curves in that direction too. The novel is fun to read, and Clement's theme of new knowledge is expressed beautifully here in the following paragraph (chapter thirteen) that also refers to Gizona's superior intellectual gifts:

> Actually, it was the same sort of drive that was to urge explorers and scientists of later centuries, [the narrative point of view in the book is definitely looking back from our time, hence some ahistorical details like the map seeing noted above] and which had already driven men across seas and mountains and deserts to learn new things. It was the urge to fill in the blank places on the picture of the world that every man keeps in his head, and which Gizona painted so much more clearly than most.

TWO NOVELS ABOUT EARTH

It would be expected that anyone who is as much a problem solver as Clement would eventually turn the pieces in the puzzle around and try them the other way. He actually did this in a novel-length fiction, which was first published as a three-part serial in *Astounding* in 1953, just before the advent of the planet novels that puzzled so successfully over the varieties of alien environments. *Iceworld* reverses the pattern—before it had been established—and explores the puzzles in the environment of Earth (the frozen planet) from the point of view of alien scientists. There is some irony in this reversal as the reader looks at the physical characteristics of his own familiar world through the eyes of creatures who marvel at the possibility of intelligent life, or any organic activity at all, on a planet with such a devastatingly low temperature range and high atmospheric pressure as compared to their home planet. Clement's literary use of the reversal in this case, however, emphasizes less the irony of difference and more the sheer excitement of discovery. As much as any of his long fictions, *Iceworld* is an exercise in the gradual uncovering of the biochemistry and atmospheric makeup of a planet. However, in this case the information to be revealed is the familiar data about free and active oxygen; atmospheric pressure of what we call one atmosphere; boiling points of liquids and especially our prime liquid, water, which the aliens call hydrogen oxide; and other details from high-school science.

Although Clement cleverly bootlegs a lot of earth science as he manages to do in all his fictions, the alien point of view and the alien's wonder at the peculiar characteristics on Planet Three of our system interest the reader more than earth science, and as the aliens gradually deduce the nature of our environment, we learn about their environment at home as the base point of reference. According to their testimony, the small planet Sarr orbits a star that is much hotter than our Sun at about 200 parsecs from the Solar System. Sarrian drug runners have discovered our tobacco plant, however, which instantly becomes a gaseous addictive mixture in their environment, and are smuggling it across the galaxy back to Sarr. A Sarrian narcotics agent, Sallman Ken, is sent to our Solar System to stop this drug traffic. He is more scientist than detective, though, and what should be a space-opera task of law enforcement stretches into a Clement tale of planet exploration and the analysis of a new and strange environment.

Sarrians have been puzzled in particular by what they observe from their space ships as the "flatlands" on Earth which seem to comprise at least two thirds of the frozen planet. They are astounded to discover through the investigations of Ken that a planet is able to hold in a liquid state enough of the compound that they analyze as hydrogen oxide to make up these flatlands. The temperature range on Sarr is high enough and the atmospheric pressure is low enough that there is very little liquid of any compound (certainly not water) in their home environment. The reader learns that on Sarr active free sulphur in the atmosphere is the equivalent of free oxygen on Earth and that the "water" on Sarr and in their living organisms consists of "copper chloride, lead bromide, and sulfides of phosphorous and potassium." It sounds as though a visit to Sarr would be like a visit to Milton's Hell, except for the fact that Sarrian scientists are pleasant enough characters. The following short exchange (chapter twelve) between Ken and one of his fellows over the strange properties of hydrogen oxide illustrates the fascination in this point-of-view reversal as a means of learning both about earth science and about the importance of assuming difference:

> "You've seen the solid form [ice], which sublimed in a near vacuum. Three has a respectable atmospheric pressure, and there may be a liquid phase of the compound. If you see any pools of any sort of liquid whatever, I would advise keeping clear of them."
> "Sound enough—only, if the planet is anything like Sarr, there isn't a chance in a thousand of landing near open liquid."
> "Our troubles seem to spring mostly from the fact that this planet *isn't* anything like Sarr," Feth pointed out drily.

The point-of-view reversal is fun, but the overall effect from *Iceworld* does not seem as powerful, either in the communicating of science or in the embedding of the theme of variety and difference, as the effect of the planet novels. It is better to go to Mesklin and to marvel at that environment (a frozen planet from our point of view) by getting as close as fiction can take us than to learn about Mesklin from explorers come to Earth. Clement arrived at that conclusion himself in the fifties.

In the late sixties in *Star Light*, Clement had divided civilizations into those that have passed their Energy Crisis (some unsuccessfully) and those that have not yet reached it. [55] Although *Star Light* itself is a satisfying example of Clement's ability to extrapolate fantastic worlds that are also scientifically plausible and interesting, he has turned more and more in his fiction since the mid-sixties to complications in Earth's own confrontation with its energy crisis. *Ocean on Top*, which was serialized in 1967 and later published in book form in 1973, is a novel about the energy shortage on Earth in the near future. Clement was to publish a much more successful extrapolation about energy on Earth, *The Nitrogen Fix* in 1980, continuing the twenty-year concern with this issue in his short fiction. However, *Ocean on Top* does contain some accomplishments and attempts that should be noticed.

First of all, the book is his only long fiction told by a first-person narrator. Other "asides" in the narrative illustrate Clement's self-conscious concern about writing "literature" rather than just doing scientific extrapolations.

Over his long career, Clement has never been absolutely confident about matters such as style, point of view, and the expression of meaning and significance. In spite of this lack of confidence, however, and sometimes almost because of it, there is a coherence of meaning and a coherence of tone running through all his work that it is one purpose of this study to describe. Clement is the naive and serious investigator whose continual interest in methodology takes him to similar conclusions, and similarly unified conclusions, about the nature of our contingent existence, as the most sophisticated literary stylists. More about these overall effects at the conclusion of this study, but here the narrative attempts in *Ocean on Top* reveal much about the seriousness and the awkwardness, at times, of Clement's literary intentions.

The narrator is an investigator for the world government Power Board, and the novel is his "report" on an eight-year-old maverick community that has secretly developed the technology for living totally independent of the diminishing world power supply. The community is at the bottom of the ocean. The narrator is a bit self-conscious throughout that his report will read as incoherent or incomplete in places. One problem is the language problem. There is no speech in the undersea community, only an intricate sign language and a kind of written shorthand, which fascinates Clement the language extrapolator. One of the narrator's frequent protestations, however, about his lack of literary polish coheres nicely with this issue of the strange language habits in the community. Near the end of chapter twelve, he interjects:

> I've never appreciated the gift of speech so much in my life. Those of you who feel, after finishing this report, that I should have learned certain key facts sooner than I did will please remember this difficulty. I don't say I shouldn't have been quicker, but I do claim some excuse for failure.

Often in his fiction, Clement will allude to a fear of failure in producing the proper literary effect. He is nervous about his writing. The other self-conscious literary issue in this novel has to do with the narrator's insistence that he is not writing realistic twentieth-century fiction, nor does he use analytic tools for a literature of character. Several times in his report, the narrator insists that he is not a psychiatrist, nor a psychologist, and that talk about the subconscious is about as meaningful to him as the "sloppy thinking" of astrology. Regardless of how close the point of view of this narrator is to Clement himself, the protestations about directness are both consistent with all of Clement's thought and, at the same time, ironically juxtaposed to his value of clever indirection.

Instead of character development, the best fictional material here is the uncovering of strange details about the environment, as is typical of Clement. In fact, the two points of suspense that drive the narrative are simply the question of how the community works and whether the narrator will decide to stay. Indeed the action is much like that in B. F. Skinner's *Walden Two* although the strong personality of a Frazier is missing from Clement's narrative. [56] *Ocean on Top* puzzles out a utopia of technology and of physiology. The most effective image in the novel ties it to Clement's strongest work in the planet novels and in his other fictions set off the Earth. Humans are surgically altered to live in the undersea environment. Thus in that sense their physiology, their language habits, and even their community become alien. Clement extrapolates, then, on the differences in physiology and in behavior so that, though the novel is set on Earth, it communicates images of variability in environment and in life. One thing that the altered humans must be careful not to do is laugh. When the narrator accidentally comes on a risible situation in chapter fifteen, he is told (by means of the intricate sign and written language), "Careful. With liquid in your lungs, laughing can kill you. They cut a key nerve in your coughing reflex when they changed you, but you can still laugh if you're not careful." Despite the danger of choking to death and the peculiar language problems, the narrator does decide to remain in the community. Clement makes a half-hearted attempt at some love motivation in the plot as an explanation, but the real reason is that even on Earth an alien environment, where liquid oxygen is absorbed by diffusion directly into the lungs, seems more interesting than the mundane world.

VI.

CHARACTERISTIC THEMES IN SHORTER FICTIONS

Writers generally begin their work with short forms, apprentice tasks to prepare them for what is to come. In the case of Hal Clement, his early scientific training at Harvard and his preparation as a fan reader of science fiction must have been superb because at least two of his early short works, written while he was still an undergraduate, can be included with some of his best later fiction as representative of the main vision of all his work. I discussed his first published story, "Proof" (1942), in chapter one as an example of his ironic and daring approach to extrapolation. I will discuss first in this chapter the novelette, "Impediment," that appeared in *Astounding* in 1942 a few months after the short story. I will then consider briefly a few other early stories and a few selected pieces of short fiction from later in Clement's career to understand further what I believe are central concerns for all his work in science fiction.

One result of the absence of a spoken language in the undersea world of *Ocean on Top* is that the tone of irony in ordinary speech must be conveyed solely through the written shorthand that has been developed by the community. Early in chapter seventeen, the narrator observes, "It's curious how hard it is to convey irony by the written word alone." [57] Actually, all literature and especially fiction, which is very seldom performed orally, struggles in a similar way over the expression of irony in language. Clement's novelette, "Impediment," is about communication between humans and aliens. Specifically, it is about language as a means of communication as opposed to direct communication through something like telepathy. A crew of strange aliens, creatures that look like huge moths, have landed on Earth looking for a particular nutriment, and they are also interested in communication with the intelligent inhabitants they find. The only problem is that the mothmen communicate by the direct perception of nerve configurations, that is mind reading. Thus the human, Kirk, whom their spokescreature (Talker) gets to know, must actually teach the system of symbols we call language to understand them. Kirk cannot read Talker's mind although Kirk's thoughts are easily perceived by the aliens. Clement's ironic title, then, works several ways. Kirk has an "impediment" to communication because he lacks telepathy. The conversations between Kirk and Talker develop hesitantly, as speech therapist to mute, although by the conclusion of their relatively short association they talk fairly well. But most drastic is Talker's basic impediment. He will never be a creature who is comfortable with language because the basic communication mode of his speech is telepathic. Thus the mothmen have the real speech "impediment."

In his "Author's Afterword" to *The Best of Hal Clement*, which reprints the novelette, Clement talks about his "innate conservatism" or doubts. [58] He also says that he is a "crass materialist." I shall leave a resolution to the question of Clement's metaphysics until my concluding chapter because, whatever version of materialist he may be, the more general question of methodology, or how to proceed in knowing about things, runs throughout his fictions about exploration and knowledge. The fact that this short work, his second published fiction, delves as deeply as it does into his notions about language, epistemology, and the advantages in limited and accumulative knowledge indicates the seriousness of his work. From the Harvard Yard (though he was a commuter student from Cambridge) through *The Nitrogen Fix*, which is set significantly around a far future Boston area, Clement's speculations in fiction have a profound unity and seriousness of purpose.

What bothers him about the telepathic, or direct, communication of information (whether it is the mothmen's telepathy here or the hive memory of the Observers in his latest novel) is that it is too perfect and thus closed. He prefers the general-purpose code system of a language. Language must be learned gradually, and there is always the danger of mistranslation from speaker to hearer—even when a speaker speaks to himself or herself internally. But a general-purpose code system allows continual new combinations and hence continual new knowledge. The greatest irony is that in an impediment, or limited knowledge, there is strength. And conversely, the absolutist or non-doubter, such as a mothman telepath, has the largest impediment. Even Clement's sophomore language in this early story captures the irony well. Perhaps the finest example comes near the conclusion when Kirk communicates to Talker his realization finally of where the greatest impediment in communication lies and, ironically, where the strength in language lies:

> Your people all "think" alike—so far as either of us is able to tell what thought is. The patterns you broadcast are mutually intelligible to members of your race, but not to me, because you have received those waves from others of your kind from earliest childhood, and I am a stranger. But my people do not communicate in that fashion . . . . The activity that occurs in our brains is never directly transmitted to other brains—it is first "coded" and then broadcast . . . . From birth, each human brain is isolated, can be reached only through the means of communication natural to us; there is no reason that all should develop alike.

As Kirk's lesson to Talker illustrates and as we have seen frequently in this study, Clement likes to speculate profoundly about the limited conditions imposed on life—and about the variable conditions of all matter. As part of this seriousness, he also has a tendency to be somewhat wordy. Clement is no Hemingway of tight compression, and when a theme interests him, such as the notions about language mentioned above, he will develop the theme in words rather than try to compress a communication of the theme into a gesture or a detail of economically worded description. This is not to say that Clement writes essays rather than fictions. There are few symbols in literature, I think, more effective for the communication of what I have called variability than the planet Mesklin of the life forms on Abyormen. But short fiction is not Clement's strongest form. He himself has published only one collection of short stories, in addition to the book of three novelettes that includes "Impediment," *Natives of Space* (1965). A few other stories have been gathered by Lester del Rey in *The Best of Hal Clement*, but Clement's most effective work is in the longer fictions.

UNCANNINESS: AFLOAT ON A FULL SEA

One of the unities that links Clement's best stories, which also flows over to the novels as we have seen, is the notion of the strangeness or non-anthropocentric nature of space. This notion is beautifully imaged in the necessary and given image for all science of variable gravity. The circular of orbital "point of turn," when gravitational forces tip a body, provides the urgency that drives many of Clement's stories. He does seem to realize the potential in the image of gravity more than most science-fiction writers although the image is part of the environment throughout the genre—and in mundane fiction as well if a writer wished to notice it. (Pynchon's *Gravity Rainbow* is a fully realized mainstream novel as well as science fiction.) Gravity can image the need for action, as momentum carries a body one way or another. Gravity also images the essential alienness or strangeness of all existence since the human point of view has gotten so accustomed to only one gravity, as Clement develops in his juvenile about the Ranger boys, whereas near infinite variations from free fall to Mesklin are the true measures of the contingency of life.

Such variety and uncertainty is both frightening and comic from the human perspective. The critic Harold Bloom has written a penetrating discussion of the tonal effects of what he calls the "poetic sublime" in which he builds much of his argument around Freud's 1919 essay on the "Uncanny." [59] In his own hard science and artistically uncertain manner, Clement creates the awe-inspiring and sublimely disorienting effects of the "uncanny" in a number of his fictions. And he accomplishes this often with details in a consideration of gravity or with the more explicit evocation of the way in which variable gravity can disorient humans. The 1947 story "Answer" which was also discussed in chapter one above, actually links images of man's disorientation in free fall with the word "uncanny." This linkage is no doubt accidental since Clement has expressed no interest whatsoever in reading Freud; thus the conjunction is further evidence of the necessity of the ideas regardless of whether readers want to yoke them in this manner. In any case, the computer in the story is an analog computer, which was a bad guess on Clement's part in the forties. [60] But the super-human capabilities of the machine disorient the visiting psychologist even more than free fall does, and Clement's term for the disorientation here is Freudian: " . . . it reflected on the entire device an aura of uncanniness that affected even Wren."

An aura of uncanniness, which makes the reader half laugh and half shudder, can be created when men are trapped in strange environments and hence are made to feel unusual. A tightly written short story that Clement is particularly proud of because the resolution of the story turns on a scientific suggestion that he has made about the behavior of dust particles on the Moon, "Dust Rag" (1956), begins with an image for man's disorientation once he is off his home planet. [61] Before the electrically charged dust particles obscure their vision, the two astronauts look back toward the Earth: " . . . the thin crescent of their home world was too close to the sun to be seen easily, and Earth doesn't look very 'human' from outside in any case."

Another story set on the Moon, which like "Dust Rag" makes use of physical lunar conditions that Clement had earlier used in his juvenile about the Ranger boys (ideas from that novel that Clement himself downgrades keep reappearing in other fictions of his), is entitled "Mistaken from Granted" and did not appear in print until 1974 although it had been used orally by Clement in scouting work for a number of years. [62] The published story is longer than it should be for good narrative effect (orally it must have been shorter), but the lengthening in a narrative is often included by Clement so that he can discuss the calculation of gravitational effects which, in turn, have human meanings in his work. The opening paragraph of this story is representative:

> People can usually get used to the weightlessness of space flight during the days or weeks it takes to cross from one world to another. In a long orbit it is easy to convince oneself that one's ship is not about to fall onto anything, even though the sensation of weight-lessness is that of endless falling. There simply is nothing visible nearby to hit. Of course, travelers have had nervous breakdowns in spaceships too badly designed to let them see out.

One of Clement's most effective short fictions, in which the pace of the narra-tive does not seem burdened with excessive extrapolation, is "Bulge" (1968), and paradoxically this story contains as much literary allusion as any of Cle-ment's work. The struggle of the old spaceman, Mac Hoerwitz, to outwit crimi-nals who have landed on the asteroid he tends is laced through with references to a number of Shakespeare's plays. Hoerwitz entertains himself in his lonely job by watching "scanner-sheets" of Shakespeare. As usual, Clement is self-conscious about his own literary competence in these latter days of technology and science fiction. One of Hoerwitz's first thoughts when the criminals in-vade his operation is that "Shakespeare would have made him [the leader of the gang] more complicated and more believable." Also, the plot in this story turns on gravity. First of all, Hoerwitz himself has the job of tending the aster-oid, which is a kind of celestial gas station set in a highly elliptical earth orbit, because of the advantage of low gravity to his old age: "He was eighty-one years old and had a mass of just one hundred pounds distributed along his seventy inches of height. He could not possibly have lifted that mass against Earth's gravity." Secondly, Hoerwitz is able momentarily to outsmart his captors because he understands and can use the essentially non-human motions of anticipating angular momentum in low gravity. But the final solution to Hoerwitz's problem in the story alludes to a passage in Shakespeare that most effectively and beautifully images the meaning of gravity, I think, for Clement. When the asteroid is approaching the perigee of its orbit, Hoerwitz happens to be watching *Julius Caesar* to lessen his pain from the torture of the gangsters. What he hears gives him the idea for finally nudging the robber's ship just off the asteroid at the exact point of perigee when the tidal forces are exactly suffi-cient to give him that edge. Although Clement does not identify the actual passage except to say it is a speech by Brutus and he does not quote the pas-sage, the following lines are undoubtedly a prime expression of the phases of change and of the sense of contingency that are so vital to Clement's vision and to his tentative work. Brutus says:

We, at the height, are ready to decline.
There is a tide in the affairs of men
Which taken at the flood leads on to fortune;
Omitted, all the voyage of their life
Is bound in shallows and in miseries.
On such a full sea are we now afloat,
And we must take the current when it serves,
Or lose our ventures.

(Act IV, scene III)

In Clement's work, the full sea on which we float is all of space. The various tides are the gravitational forces, and fiction is possible because of both the uncertainty and the urgency of the tidal flow.

FROM EXOBIOLOGY TO GENETIC ENGINEERING

The story of Mac Hoerwitz is a well-paced adventure, and the central character is one of the fuller adult characters in Clement's work because of the urgency of what he must do. Although the gravity of human action and of the action for any life form is an important matter in all of Clement's fiction, speculation about the myriad forms life may take within the myriad possible physical environments that an extrapolator can imagine is equally important. Moral decision making and biological evolution may intersect at the point of genetic engineering finally. But in Clement's ficton, as we have seen, biological speculation has a special place long before he begins to write about the Energy Crisis.

"Uncommon Sense" (1945) is Clement's first short piece to contain exobiological speculation in which the strange alien environment determines an unusual life form. The aliens in both "Proof" and "Impediment" are more like spokesmen for unusual environments. The reader never *sees* them at home. But the unnamed, hot planet in orbit around the supergiant star, Deneb, is very real for Cunningham, the exobiologist explorer, and his mutinous crew in this story. Clement has admitted that Donald Menzel, his astronomy professor, with whom he had argued over the type of sense perception that he speculates into this Denebian environment, would have had further objections. Menzel would not have believed that planets could be posited for such a massive center of radiation as Deneb. [63] Also, the star itself is in the same portion of our galaxy as the Mesklinite worlds and Tenebra, which indicates that the germ may have been created in this story that later blossomed into Clement's peopling of that portion of the sky five parsecs from Earth toward the Cygnus and Aquila Constellations. In any case, the hot-life form that Cunningham discovers and accurately analyzes here possesses a synesthesia-type sense as interesting as that of the hot creatures on Abyormen and foreshadowing the thirty-five years and more of Hal Clement's speculations about exobiology:

. . . that was just what those "eyes" did. In the nearly perfect vacuum of this little world's surface, gases diffused at high speed— and their molecules traveled in practically straight lines. There was nothing wrong with the idea of a pinhole camera eye, whose retina was composed of olefactory nerve endings rather than the rods and cones of photosensitive organs . . . . Every substance, solid or liquid, has its vapor pressure; under Deneb's rays even some rather unlikely materials probably evaporated enough to affect the organs of these life forms—metals, particularly. The life fluid of the creatures was obviously metal . . . .

Two Clement short stories, "Halo" (1952) and "The Foundling Stars" (1966), speculate about alien life forms so large in size, those in the first occupying nearly as much space as the Earth, that biological details about them are not well realized since their environments seem to be the nebulosity of open space itself. But most of his remaining short pieces, as well as many of the ones already discussed, treat only humans in unusual environments. In other words, Clement apparently has preferred the novel-length for the full development of exobiology. One late story, however, does continue his development of unusual aliens in the context of their unusual environments. "Stuck with It" (1976) can also be seen as a transition to Clement's other later work, such as *Ocean on Top* that contains his continuing debate about nature versus nurture, about technology and the Energy Crisis, and about biological engineering as both a solution and a contributing factor to the Energy Crisis.

Laird Cunningham, the same exobiologist as in "Uncommon Sense," finds himself in this later story on a planet that he has named Ranta, from the Finnish word for shore or shoreline, because much of the world is always under water in intertidal zones. [64] The story itself also can be seen as on several edges or shores of Clement's fiction. The native Rantans are massive snake-like creatures, and Cunningham speculates throughout the story about the origins of their intelligence and culture as it has been apparently influenced by the tides. As it turns out, the Rantans are shrewd and secretive like the Mesklinites (as Clement undoubtedly remembers his earlier work) so that it is not until after they have insinuated some new knowledge from Cunningham that he and the reader can finally penetrate their scientific and technological concerns. What they learn is how to make wagons, which is a real breakthrough for their water-bound culture, so that they can move more easily on land. What Cunningham learns is that the Rantans paradoxically are suffering from technological pollution caused not by chemical or mechnical engineering but by biological engineering. They have used too much genetic engineering, and they want to return to "nature." The story concludes with Cunningham and his Rantan friends discussing the question of nature versus nurture or technology, which is an issue lurking always at the shoreline or edge of science, that Clement has written about often in the past decade and a half. Cunningham says:

> Once you tip the balance, you never get quite back on dead center. You started a scientific culture, just as my people did. You got overdependent on your glue [a living organism they engineered], just as we did on heat engines . . . . You still want to get back to your tidal jungles, I suppose. Maybe you will . . . . In any case, it will take you a long, long time to get around that circle; and you'll learn a lot of things on the way; and believe it or not, the trip will be fun.

Cunningham's final emphasis here on the "fun" of problem solving is so characteristic of Clement that even when his later stories and his most recent novel, *The Nitrogen Fix*, deal with the serious issues of the Energy Crisis and genetic engineering, his tone is playful and adventuresome. For example, two fascinating novelettes from the mid-sixties make use of genetic engineering in an Earth environment in elaborate speculations. Both were apparently written when Clement was beginning to take up the concept of the Energy Crisis as a watershed for civilizations as he set forth the idea in *Star Light* and both to prepare the way for *The Nitrogen Fix*. "Raindrop" (1965) postulates an enclosed body of water, at least five miles in diameter, in orbit around the Earth and contained by a living skin of "gelatin-capsule algae" genetically engineered for the purpose. Not only is this satellite raindrop a weightless aquarium for the rapid evolution and harvesting of aquatic foodstuffs, but also it is a brilliant image for the continual sense of falling and hanging in a kind of "limbo" that reminds the reader of Clement's favorite image of gravity.

Finally, "The Mechanic" (1966) contains examples of biological engineering developed in the Earth's oceans that actually reappear in nearly the same forms in *The Nitrogen Fix*. A few android zeowhales made to harvest copper out of sea water are still "living" as part of the pseudolife after the ecological disaster that sets the scene for the later novel. Including a central character with the name of Clement's son, Rick Stubbs, the story is a delightful and almost playful extrapolation on the engineering of biological forms—including Stubbs himself. One detail in the story, however, may be an ominous foreshadowing of what can go wrong with genetic engineering and is a good place to conclude this chapter that has dealt with characteristic traits in Clement's short fiction ranging from the fantastic extrapolation of alien life in alien environments to the human centered concern with the environment of Earth. The careful selection of biological properties to be engineered is exactly what goes wrong in the world of *The Nitrogen Fix*, and the following passage suggests how sexual reproduction, of all things in Clement, could result in a loss of control over biological properties:

> The zeowhales and their kindred devices reproduced asexually; the genetic variation magnification, which is the biological advantage of sex, was just what the users of the pseudoorganisms did not want, at least until some factor could be developed which would tend to select for the characteristics they wanted most.

In other words, sex produces too much variation to control properly. The working out of the tonal effect of this idea will have to be seen in *The Nitrogen Fix*. Clement himself leaves a shrewd trail.

VII.

NITROGEN AND BEYOND

Like Clement's own fascination with orbits and circling, the inclination of this study was to discuss his most recent novel *The Nitrogen Fix* initially in the first chapter along with an introduction to his favorite themes. It remains only to reiterate to conclude. Also, the considerable amount of resonance in *The Nitrogen Fix* makes it an ideal summation and, perhaps even, fulfillment to the best of Clement's fiction to date. Critical studies must not presume, however, to serve as roadmaps for writers to show them where to go next. They can map where a writer has been, and Clement's career pauses nicely at this most recent novel. It is a major new work that picks up and vibrates with many of his most effective themes and ideas.

Clement has said that he worked on this novel for nearly twenty years, and many of the seeds of the story can be seen in his novelettes of the sixties about Earth's energy crisis. [65] For example, the marine pseudolife produced by genetic engineering that the nomad family in the novel still make use of to harvest copper from the acid oceans is described in detail in "The Mechanic." As we saw in the previous chapter, sexual reproduction for this pseudolife is an issue with Clement. In the novel, the analogy between sex and communication plays a key role (discussed in chapter one). Similarly, both the novelette and the novel seem to exist very close to Harry Stubbs himself. The protagonist in "The Mechanic" is named Rick Stubbs, and the novel is set in the Boston area with specific reference to places such as Milton and Blue Hill where Harry Stubbs (the real Hal Clement) lives and works. [66] But most importantly, the topic of major and catastrophic change in the earth's environment seems to have occupied Clement's thought during the sixties and seventies. He wrote often about the Energy Crisis ("Raindrop," *Ocean on Top*, the scheme of a crisis point for every civilization detailed in *Star Light*) and about the efforts of science to deal with the environment on Earth.

The Nitrogen Fix tells the story of a scientific blunder (a fix or predicament) on a grand scale. Apparently, through the biological engineering of microbes intended to improve agriculture, science had begun sometime in the future an accelerating process of "fixing" free oxygen from the atmosphere into nitrogen compounds. By the time of the novel, this process has produced (presumably in addition to more fertilizer at first) catastrophic results. The oceans have become solutions of nitric acid (weak but still able to yellow the skin). Numerous nitrogen compounds behave explosively and unpredictably. Worst of all only a trace of free oxygen remains in the atmosphere. Plant life in the open has evolved to nitrogren life that produces its energy by reducing nitrates (often explosively). The only oxygen animal life remaining on Earth are the small colonies of humans who carefully produce breathable air from plants in underground cities. A few nomads live as outcasts in the open air of the nitrogen atmosphere, and the story follows the primitive technology of survival of one nomad family.

The alien Observers (a nitrogen-life animal species), named Bones by the nomads, also figure prominently in the story; they were the main focus of my discussion of the novel in chapter one. Along with the Observers, the reader is intrigued to discover what happened to Earth. To conclude the narrative, Clement offers a possibility for the reversal of the chemical and biological process. Microbes are being developed by biological engineering that will release free oxygen from nitrogen compounds back into the atmosphere. Although the time scale for these processes is not clear, the hope finally is that in the future open air photosynthesis and blue skies (rather than yellow) may return to Earth. If that were to happen, the Observer species would move on to learn from another nitrogen environment. Clement broadens the action of the novel by suggesting that the Observer species, motivated exclusively by curiosity, travels the galaxy watching this peculiar "fixing" of free oxygen into nitrogen compounds on one planet after another. Earth is the only planetary environment, in fact, within the hive memory of the species where the process has the possibility of being reversed.

The significant resonance in this novel, however, derives from the image of catastrophic environmental change and what causes it. Not only does science overstep itself in biological engineering, but also Clement images the traditional notion of decline from a Golden Age as well as the notion of mankind alone and himself an alien in his own home environment. First of all, the central family of nomads in the novel, wandering on their raft, reminds the reader somewhat of the Huck Finn condition of an earlier period of American self-reliance. The name of the family, in fact, is Fyn. Secondly, the notion of lost Golden Ages appears in the story almost by surprise. It deepens and enriches a pathos in Clement's work that is associated, I believe, with the idea of limited knowledge and seen most effectively earlier in *Cycle of Fire*; however, the reader does not expect it. We do not absolutely need to know what enzyme accelerates the oxygen-fixation reaction in the originally engineered microbes, but the narrative hints at this bit of information often until Clement reveals at the end of chapter nineteen that the real culprit is gold. Just before the name of the metal is revealed, one of the Observers explains why it has always seemed strange to the scientific curiosity of his/her species that the widespread distribution of gold should immediately precede the ecological change to nitrogen life—in the case of Earth, a grand ecological disaster following an age of gold:

> I have not been able to learn why it is so widespread in every planet's crust. It is one of the standing mysteries, which presents itself on world after world. It is a highly unreactive metal, which I would expect to find uncombined and highly localized. It should *not* be so thoroughly spread through a planet's soil and crust that a microbe can count on finding enough of its atoms whenever it needs them for its personal chemistry. One hypothesis is that a scientific race used and scattered it, but there has been no way to tell; I have never found a use for it myself, except in the most limited quantities in the laboratory.

For the devoted fan of Hal Clement, the decline from a Golden Age may seem like an unusual image. He can't be that circular and nonprogressive in his thinking. It must be just an unlucky image. The images about epistemology, scientific method, and language as they appear in the alien psychology of Bones and in the human character development are more familiar images. But here too the themes are reversed, and the images are deepened. Resonance is, indeed, significant in this latest novel, and the reader who knows much of Clement's earlier work is best prepared to understand. The Fyn family members, even though they are self-reliant nomads, rely on a methodology just the reverse of Mesklinite experimentation. They are afraid to try anything new, and custom and habit are better guides to action for them than thinking. In fact, after the ecological disaster that destroyed oxygen life on the surface of the Earth, words like "experiment" and "invent" have become taboo words. One of the main actions of the novel is the gradual discovery by the humans that innovative thinking can be useful. Thus, on the one hand, the Observer psychology explores the limited knowledge even in the direct communication of thought and, on the other hand, the human characters must learn gradually to overcome a deep anti-science bias.

Finally, the deepest reversal in methodology in the novel (though it may be seen simply as an extension of Clement's notion of accumulating more knowledge from partial knowledge) is that the hesitant experimentation, which finally will offer the possibility of returning Earth to a habitable environment, is performed by a young group of city dwellers who are violent in behavior and fanatically wrong in many of their hypotheses. In other words, the Observers in their oneness and compulsive curiosity are the truly rational creatures in this story whereas progress and potentially beneficial change is brought about by a group of irrational men who are patently wrong about the past. The Hillers or city dwellers who "invent" the new microbe believe fanatically that the Observer species has destroyed the earth's atmosphere. Clement's skill in this latest novel to reverse roles and to suggest ironic depths of action is significant.

Prior to the advent of modern chemistry, the word for nitrogen gas was "azote"—or "not live." (Actually, this was Lavoisier's term because he could not support life with the gas.) Clement's latest novel, in a sense, is about the ambiguities of a death/life situation. The most interesting characters in the book are the nitrogen-life Observers, or Bones. At the end of the story, they are helpful in protecting the rebels who are developing the proper mechanism to return a habitable environment to Earth. Thus, not only does the solution come from a group that is violently mistaken about many things, but also the nitrogen, or "death," life assists in bringing the vitality of free oxygen back to earth's atmosphere.

Ambiguities like these are essential to a Golden-Age/Iron-Age vision of progress. Ideas that I think have been latent in Clement's work all along are brought to explicit expression in this novel where gold is the culprit and progress or the solution of problems is complex. The classical Iron Age was certainly a degenerate time compared to the glories of the Golden Age. But paradoxically in an Iron Age, progress can take place—even more so than in a Golden Age when development is more or less static because of the utopian conditions (note the pure rationality of the Observers as compared to the confusion of the humans, but the humans do invent the new microbe). And progress always occurs in an Iron Age when less than golden means are used. Clement's version of this paradox reflects his belief that limited, partial knowledge is the best source of accumulating knowledge. Here the paradox is made more explicit (and related to Gold) in the fact that the anti-science and the abhorrence of experimentation eventually gives way to what will probably be the correct solution even in the Nitro Age after the catastrophe, and the death life of nitrogen will eventually lead to the vitality of real life, as we oxygen creatures know it, on Earth again.

BEYOND MATERIALISM

In spite of what he says in the "Author's Afterword" to *The Best of Hal Clement* about being a "crass materialist," Clement's presentation of complexity, mystery, and the ironic surprise is done too consistently throughout his career not to suggest a contextual reality in his thinking that is greater than the sum of its parts. [67] Even the Observers in *The Nitrogen Fix* comment that they have never encountered a planet where the progress toward nitrogen life (or decline) has been reversed, and yet the movement in the novel is toward just such a reversal. Mysterious possibilities and ironic changes certainly can be part of the mechanism of matter, which is far from simple, but they also suggest something beyond. To say the least, Clement's materialism is never a mechanistic materialism. He is too interested in mind and in the problems of epistemology for that. Although he never speculates about anything other than a physical matrix for communication and for thinking, the varieties and changes in mental activity that he works into his stories suggest the importance and the ultimate mystery of mind to him. In other words, the mental complexities he likes to write about are seldom reducible to stimulus-and-reaction relationships. There is something unpredictable about Mesklinite shrewdness, Abyormenite decisions to die, and even explosive nitrogen life.

Part of my argument for placing Clement's ideas beyond the reductions of materialism is based on his continual awareness of man's disorientation and the tone of ironic acceptance of this disorientation in his work. Somehow Clement knows that mankind is the ultimate alien species. He knows that we must cope, and learn, and that by such means we can progress. But finally mankind will always feel disoriented and out of place in a way that matter would never "feel" in a material universe. The nervous laugh of the narrator in a Clement story (even if it is just because he is not sure of his role as literary man, such as the speculator in "Proof") coupled with the ironic variability in all of his alien environments from Mesklin to the "azote" yellow Earth speak about being slightly out of phase in the universe—always slightly falling.

But Clement, finally, is not a philosopher even though the hard science fiction he has written so well for four decades is a literature of ideas. He is a writer of fiction. (He has also written some interesting nonfiction that there has not been room enough in this study to discuss.) There is a seriousness of purpose and a unity of vision in his fiction that I have tried to describe. Further, Clement—in spite of his disclaimers laid out in my opening chapter—has pursued the art of science fiction. He has attempted different kinds of story telling, and he has invented a rich variety of settings, characters, and plots. What he may have forfeited in elegance of style (though he is always clear), he has made up in the overall resonance of his themes and ideas. He is a superb Iron-Age writer whose ever-present sense of limitation is one of his great human strengths.

NOTES

1. The number of book-length studies that treat science fiction as a serious area of literary study has actually been increasing. See Darko Suvin, *Metamorphoses of Science Fiction* (New Haven: Yale University Press, 1979) and Gary K. Wolfe, *The Known and the Unknown: The Iconography of Science Fiction* (Kent, Ohio: Kent State University Press, 1979). I am grateful to the Research Council of Kent State University for support in this study.
2. Many of Hal Clement's personal recollections and statements in this paper are from a taped interview I held with him at his home in Milton, Massachusetts, June 22, 1980, referred to henceforth as "Interview."
3. The best source for ready reference about details pertaining to all aspects of the genre from names such as John Campbell to pulp titles, such as *Astounding Science Fiction*, is Peter Nicholls, ed., *The Science Fiction Encyclopedia* (Garden City, NY: Doubleday, 1979). The title of the Asimov cover story in the June 1942 *Astounding* is "Bridle and Saddle."
4. Donald H. Menzel was Director of the Harvard Observatory where *Sky and Telescope* was published when Clement was there. Menzel has published

widely in the field of astronomy, but I can find no listing for published science fiction of his.

5. Interview. Clement said his war experiences were not very exciting. He never saw an enemy fighter. Perhaps, instead, competent technology leads scientists to wish to escape to fiction at times.

6. Hal Clement, *First Flights to the Moon*, (Garden City, NY: Doubleday, 1970). The most reliable source for bibliographical data on the first editions of each of Clement's nearly 20 books (a couple of titles have been reissued under new titles) is L. W. Currey, *Science Fiction and Fantasy Authors: A Bibliography of First Printings of Their Fiction and Selected Nonfiction* (Boston: G. K. Hall, 1979). NESFA represents the best outcomes from fandom; and Clement has been active in the association which has published reference works, sponsored conventions, and contributed to the development of the genre.

7. Clement has said, also, that the first several hundred dollars he earned for "Proof" and "Impediment" in *Astounding* in June and in August 1942 helped his parents to take his hobby seriously. Interview.

8. Interview. Also see R. Reginald, *Contemporary Science Fiction Authors II* (Detroit: Gale, 1979), p. 856.

9. Ibid.

10. Letter from Harry C. Stubbs (Hal Clement) to the author, dated July 23, 1979.

11. James Gunn, "I. Asimov," *Extrapolation*, 21 (Winter, 1980), 311. Asimov writes hard science fiction, but his work is neither as complex nor as interesting as Clement's though his overall writing career has been widely and justly acclaimed.

12. Clement, *The Nitrogen Fix* (New York: Ace Books, 1980).

13. Interview.

14. For love and sex in science fiction, see the work of Theodore Sturgeon or Philip Jose Farmer, although Walter Tevis's recent novel *Mockingbird* (1980) is a beautiful love story with some sex.

15. *The Nitrogen Fix*, pp. 208-209.

16. Clement, "Answer," *The Best of Hal Clement*, ed. Lester del Rey (New York: Ballantine Books, 1979), p. 170.

17. For this novel, Clement has written a non-fiction explanation of the planetary conditions. See "Author's Afterword: Whirligig World," *Mission of Gravity* (Boston: Gregg Press, 1978), pp. 242-256.

18. See *Close to Critical* (1964), *Star Light* (1971), and "Stuck With It" (1976) in *Best of....*

19. At the conclusion of the novel, *The Nitrogen Fix*, the humans and the aliens are on the road to making a reducing culture that will restore free oxygen to the atmosphere. The aliens, then, presumably will depart for other planets since they are nitro-life.

20. See *Needle* (1950), *Iceworld* (1953), and especially *Through the Eye of a Needle* (1978) in addition to several stories in *Small Changes* (1969).

21. Interview. The article is Andre Lwoff, "The Life Cycle of a Virus," *Scientific American*, 190 (March 1954), 34-37. Lwoff is almost poetic in talking about death, life cycles, and order and disorder so that one can understand why the article should be a fine inspiration for the poetics of variety in Clement.

22. The topic of what manner of aesthetic response nature stimulates in the perceiver has ben widely written about since the time of Edmund Burke especially.

23. Clement, "Answer," pp. 150-151.

24. Clement, *Close to Critical* (New York: Ballantine Books, 1964), p. 190.

25. Clement, "Proof," *Where Do We Go From Here: Great Science Fiction Classics,* ed. Isaac Asimov (Greenwich, CT: Fawcett, 1971), p. 135.

26. Interview.

27. Asimov and Sturgeon, both Campbell writers for *Astounding* during the forties, did not publish a book of science fiction until 1950 and 1948, respectively.

28. Interview.

29. Ibid.

30. Martin H. Greenberg, *Isaac Asimov Presents the Great SF Stories 4* (1942), ed. Martin H. Greenberg and Isaac Asimov (New York: DAW Books, 1980), p. 205.

31. Interview. Asimov, of course, is also closely linked with the detective story and has written many. More recent authors, also, have combined science fiction and mystery writing beautifully, such as Alfred Bester, Evan Hunter, and, perhaps most recently, Stephen Donaldson who publishes detective novels under the name Reed Stephens. The reasons are both the commerical ties of the two popular literatures to mass market publishing and the role of ratiocination in both.

32. Interview. Clement recalls a story by Nat Schachner that he read in the mid-thirties in *Astounding* entitled "Infra-Universe" (December 1936-January 1937). The novel by Kipling was published in 1901.

33. See Frank N. Magill, ed., *Survey of Science Fiction Literature* (Englewood Cliffs, NJ: Salem Press, 1979), III, 1505-1506. The de Camp piece is entitled "Design for Life" and may be the basis for Campbell's well-known advice not to create sympathetic aliens that led Asimov to people the galaxy with humans.

34. Interview. The Sturgeon Story was "Tiny and the Monster." It first appeared in *Astounding Science Fiction*, May 1947.

35. Henceforth in this study, quotations from science fiction will be identified by chapter in the text. Page number citations will be omitted since paperback editions vary and are often hard to locate. My practice in chapter one was to provide the model for standard bibliographic citation. The Bibliography at the end will identify the editions I have used.

36. "Assumption Unjustified" (1946).

37. See John Clute review in *Foundation* No. 16 (May 1979), pp. 105-106.

38. A valuable summary of this critical approach, which I do not wish to belabor with regard to Clement but which is useful, can be found in John Sturrock, ed., *Structuralism and Since from Levi-Strauss to Derrida* (New York: Oxford University Press, 1979).

39. "Impediment" (1942).

40. Interview.

41. Interview. He also acknowledges the greater accuracy of the MIT computers in R. Reginald, *Contemporary Science Fiction Authors II* (Detroit: Gale, 1979), p. 856.

42. "Cold Front," first published in *Astounding Science Fiction* (1946), rpt. in *Men Against the Stars*, ed. Martin Greenberg (New York: Gnome, 1950).

43. "Whirligig World," first published in *Astounding Science Fiction* (1953), later reprinted as "Author's Afterword" in most editions of the novel.

44. "Lecture Demonstration" (1973).

45. See Frank N. Magill, ed., *Survey of Science Fiction Literature* (Englewood Cliffs: Salem Press, 1979), III, 1424-1428. The critical essay is by Neil Barron.

46. Ibid. and Interview.

47. Clement has also speculated in nonfiction essays about alien solar systems that have not yet been worked into his fiction. See the essay on the Xi Bootis system that he wrote for a science-fiction convention help in Pittsburgh in the 1960's and published in pamphlet form by Advent in Chicago.

48. A minor character among the aliens is named "Oliver." Clement's use of allusion like this if often rather whimsical.

49. Interview.

50. See the note on the Lwoff article in chapter one above.

51. Barry N. Malzberg, *Galaxies* (New York: Pyramid, 1975), chapter thirteen.

52. Letter from Harry C. Stubbs (Hal Clement) to the author dated July 26, 1980. The book is hard to locate; Clement kindly gave me a copy. Also, the uncertain publication record of this book is no doubt a further reason why series are anathema to Clement. See chapter two above.

53. See the entry on "Dime Novels" in Peter Nicholls, *The Science Fiction Encyclopedia* (New York: Doubleday, 1979), p. 171.

54. A detailed comparison of Clement's expectations for astronauts to the description of Tom Wolfe in *The Right Stuff* (New York: Farrar, Straus, & Giroux, 1979) would undoubtedly reveal profound differences in tone and emphasis but a similar confidence in youth.

55. See chapter four above.

56. Skinner's utopian novel (1948) is the more effective work because of the strong character role played by his protagonists even though they are two-dimensional. See my essay on the book in Frank Magill, *Survey of Science Fiction Literature* (Englewood Cliffs: Salem Press, 1979), V, 2392-95.

57. The late 18th-century *philosophe*, Erasmus Darwin, who was both scientist and writer, speculated about the need for a punctuation mark for irony and proposed the inverted exclamation mark. See my study, *Erasmus Darwin* (New York: Twayne, 1974).

58. Lester del Rey is the compiler and editor of *The Best of Hal Clement* in the Ballantine series (New York: Ballantine, 1979).

59. See Harold Bloom, "Freud and the Poetic Sublime, A Catastrophe Theory of Creativity," *Antaeus*, 30/31 (Spring 1978), 335-377. Bloom's work as well as the work of some of the structuralist critics hovers often just at the edge of this study, and I think a systematic application of more contemporary thought on literary theory to the better science fiction would not be inappropriate.

60. Clement has acknowledged that he was wrong, along with many others, in the forties about the near total manner in which the digital computer has come to dominate the field. Clement freely acknowledges scientific miscalculations he may make, no doubt subscribing to Bacon's notion that more can be learned from error than from confusion.

61. In the "Author's Afterword" in *The Best of Hal Clement*, he writes, "I submitted a very brief paper to [*The Strolling Astronomer*] suggesting that electric effects might raise dust from the crater floor, and that this might also account for some anomalous occultation effects . . . . The suggestion met with a deafening silence in professional circles, but it did provide a story background."

62. The detail that appears in both fictions is the fact that the North Star, Polaris, seen from the moon is in a slightly different position relative to the moon's axis and so can deceive someone from Earth trying to move to the "north." Clement's account of the origin of this story around a campfire in scouting is also excellent and appears in the "Author's Afterword" in *The Best of Hal Clement*.

63. This is another instance where he candidly admits that his science might be a bit off the mark. See again the "Author's Afterword" in *The Best of Hal Clement*.

64. I am indebted to my Kent State University colleague, Professor Martin Nurmi, who is fluent in Finnish, for this translation.

65. Interview.

66. Approaching Clement's home in Milton, Massachusetts, I drove past Blue Hill, which in the novel is the primary domed underground city of the Hillers.

67. See the previous chapter on short fiction and the discussion of the story "Impediment."

ANNOTATED PRIMARY BIBLIOGRAPHY

This alphabetical listing states briefly the nature of each of Clement's books, including the contents of the two collections of short fiction he has published with the original years of publication of the stories noted. In addition to the first editons of his original books, the library edition of *Mission of Gravity* and the volume devoted to Clement in *The Best of . . .* series from Ballantine are also listed. The annotations are short and are intended simply to remind the reader about the contents of each book. Discussions of almost all his fictions occur in the preceding chapters of this study, and the index identifies those pages on which a book or story is mentioned.

The Best of Hal Clement. Ed. Lester del Rey. New York: Ballantine Books, 1979. Short fiction from magazines and earlier collections. Also included are an introduction by del Rey (see secondary bibliography) and Clement's "Author's Afterword."
  "Impediment" (see *Natives of Space*)
  "Technical Error" (see *Natives of Space*)
  "Uncommon Sense" (see *Small Changes*)
  "Assumption Unjustified" (see *Natives of Space*)
  "Answer" (1947): A psychologist takes the opportunity to question the ultimate computer about the true nature of mind and goes mad because of the infinite regress of the answer.
  "Dust Rag" (see *Small Changes*)
  "Bulge" (1968): The attendant of a fuel station asteroid in earth orbit gets the idea for outwitting some criminals from a Shakespeare play.
  "Mistaken for Granted" (1974): Youth on the moon miscalculates directions in a way similar to *The Ranger Boys in Space*.
  "A Question of Guilt" (1976): An historical fiction about a daring extrapolation in ancient times with the principle of blood transfusion, and with its practice, that ends in pathos.
  "Stuck With It" (1976): A mutual learning experience between a human explorer and aquatic aliens, who resemble large reed-like plants, in which shrewdness and indirection play important roles in the epistemology.
Close to Critical. New York: Ballantine Books, 1964. This novel follows the remote control teaching and management of aliens on the high pressure planet Tenebra. In addition to exploration, one of their tasks is to rescue a human adolescent, Easy Rich, and a young alien from another planet who become stranded on Tenebra.

Cycle of Fire. New York: Ballantine Books, 1957. This novel focuses on the growth of friendship and mutual enlightenment between the alien Dar Lang Ahn and the human Nils Kruger, who has been left on Dar's home planet Abyormen. In addition to learning about the changing environment on Abyormen, both learn a good deal about life, death, and methods of learning.

First Flights to the Moon. Garden City: Doubleday, 1970. This collection which contains stories by Asimov, Clarke, Niven, and others, was edited by Clement. He also contributed a foreword, notes, and an essay about the relation of science fiction to the NASA moon mission of 1969.

From Outer Space. New York: Avon, 1957. This novel is an unchanged reissue of *Needle*.

Iceworld. New York: Gnome Press, 1953. This novel is told mostly from the point of view of aliens from the extremely hot planet Sarr as they do business around Earth, a totally frozen and strange environment to them, and have first contact with a human family, the Wings.

Left of Africa. New Orleans: The Aurian Society Press, 1976. This juvenile novel follows the journey around the continent Africa in about 500 B.C. of a young Spaniard named Gizona, and also traces the learning process in his mind that leads to his independent conclusion that the Earth is round.

Mission of Gravity. Garden City: Doubleday, 1954. This novel follows the journey of Barlennan and his crew of the *Bree* across their native planet Mesklin to recover a downed human rocket at the high gravity South Pole, and also shrewdly to learn the principles of flight from the humans. Sequel: *Star Light* (see below).

Mission of Gravity. Ed. with an introduction by Poul Anderson. Boston: Gregg Press, 1978. This library edition of the novel also contains the short story about Mesklin "Lecture Demonstration" (1973) and Clement's "Author's Afterword: Whirligig World" (1953).

Natives of Space. New York: Ballantine, 1965. This collection of novelettes contains the following:

"Assumption Unjustified" (1946): an analysis of a kind of vampirism necessary for sympathetic extra-terrestrial aliens.

"Technical Error" (1944): human spacemen stranded on an asteroid must unravel the machine-tool techniques central to a deserted alien space craft.

"Impediment" (1942): communication between a telepathic alien and a human bound by language.

Needle: Garden City: Doublday, 1950. Later title: *From Outer Space* (see above). This novel describes the symbiosis between the alien detective "The Hunter" and his adopted human host Bob Kinnaird as they track down a criminal alien who has taken Bob's father as his host. Sequel: *Through the Eye of a Needle* (see below).

The Nitrogen Fix. New York: Ace, 1980. This novel follows the combined efforts of alien Observers and several groups of human survivors to understand the causes and to find a solution to the environmental catastrophe on Earth in which free oxygen in the atmosphere has been reduced to only a trace.

Ocean on Top. New York: DAW Books, 1973. This novel describes an undersea, utopian-like community that has been founded secretly as a response to the Energy Crisis on Earth. As in Skinner's *Walden Two*, the narrator has to decide whether or not to stay with the community.

The Ranger Boys in Space. Boston: L.C. Page, 1956. This juvenile novel proposes that young, orphaned boys are best suited to be astronauts because they are least adjusted to Earth and Earth gravity in a story about the first moon landing by a runaway boy.

Small Changes. Garden City: Doubleday, 1969. Also titled *Space Lash* (see below).

This collection of short fiction contains the following:

"Dust Rag" (1956): inventive thinking about the behavior of dust particles on the moon saves the lives of two astronauts.

"Sun Spot" (1960): tale of a human exploration team close to the Sun.

"Uncommon Sense" (1945): an exobiologist must deduce how creatures see in an alien environment in order to survive.

'Trojan Fall'' (1944): an escaping criminal miscalculates the "Trojan" point in orbital mechanics with disastrous results.

"Fireproof" (1969): a criminal fails to understand that convection currents will not support combustion in a microgravity environment with disastrous results.

"Halo" (1952): near planet-sized aliens use our solar system as a farm.

"The Foundling Stars" (1966): other gigantic aliens toy with human explorers.

"Raindrop" (1965): the melted nucleii of several small comets enclosed in a genetically engineered "living" skin serves as the Earth satellite setting for a story about the Energy Crisis.

"The Mechanic" (1966): another story about the Energy Crisis with details of biological and genetic engineering that appear later in *The Nitrogen Fix*.

Space Lash. New York: Dell, 1969. An unchanged reissue of *Small Changes*.

Star Light. New York: Ballantine Books, 1971. This novel is a sequel to *Mission of Gravity* in which Mesklinites under the direction of humans explore the gigantic object Dhrawn to determine if it should be classed as a planet or star; they also shrewdly wrest new knowledge from the humans. Clement's scheme of the Energy Crisis for civilizations is first analyzed here.

Through the Eye of a Needle. New York: Ballantine, 1978. This novel is a close sequel to *Needle* in which medical problems develop in the symbiosis between The Hunter and Bob and are solved in detective fashion.

ANNOTATED SECONDARY BIBLIOGRAPHY

This alphabetical listing by author includes the few critical and descriptive discussions to date of Clement's work. There are no previous book-length studies of his work. Reference to the numerous reviews of his books since 1969 can be located most easily in the annual volumes of Hal Hall's *Science Fiction Book Review Index*.

Allen, L. David. "Mission of Gravity." *Science Fiction Reader's Guide*. Lincoln: Centennial Press, 1974, pp. 103-111. This plot summary and description of the novel is not error free.

Anderson, Poul. "Introduction." *Mission of Gravity*. Boston: Gregg Press, 1978. This is a short but penetrating appreciation of all Clement's work by another master of hard science fiction.

Barlowe, Wayne Douglas, and Ian Summers. *Barlowe's Guide to Extra-Terrestrials*. New York: Workman Publishing, 1979. This volume of art also contains accurate and interesting summary descriptions of two of Clement's alien life forms: Mesklinites and the "hot" life on Abyormen.

Barron, Neil. "Mission of Gravity." In *Survey of Science Fiction Literature*. Ed. Frank N. Magill. Englewood Cliffs: Salem Press, 1979, III, 1424-1428. This critical essay makes an unnecessarily low assessment of *Star Light* in passing, but is an excellent discussion of the classic novel itself.

Clute, John. "Hal Clement." In *The Science Fiction Encyclopedia*. Ed. Peter Nicholls. Garden City: Doubleday, 1979, pp. 123-24. A short assessment of Clement's work that denies him any resonance of theme or idea.

Del Rey, Lester. "Hal Clement: Rationalist." *The Best of Hal Clement*. Ed. Lester del Rey. New York: Ballantine, 1979, pp. xi-xvii. This is a rather quirky but appreciative introduction to all of Clement's work by an old pro.

Hassler, Donald M. "Hal Clement." In *Twentieth-Century Science Fiction Writers*. Ed. Curtis Smith. New York: St. Martin's Press, 1981, pp. 117-118. A short overall assessment of his work.

—————————————. " 'Fallings from Us': The Irony of Utopia in Hal Clement and Wordsworth." *Mosaic* [India]. Special Issue on Science Fiction edited by Marshall Tymn, in press. This paper explores Clement's use of the image of gravity and Wordsworth's use of the image of falling in "Ode: Intimations of Immortality."

Meyers, Walter E. "Needle." In *Survey of Science Fiction Literature*. Ed. Frank N. Magill. Englewood Cliffs: Salem Press, 1979, III, 1505-1508. This critical essay contains several serious errors of fact and fails to recognize the resonance in the novel.

Schmidt, Stanley. "The Science in Science Ficton." In *Many Futures, Many Worlds*. Ed. Thomas D. Clareson. Kent, OH: Kent State University Press, 1977, pp. 27-49. Clement is mentioned often in this essay by a former physics teacher, science-fiction writer, and now editor of *Analog*.

Index

www.ingramcontent.com/pod-product-compliance
Lightning Source LLC
Chambersburg PA
CBHW021349090426
42742CB00008B/789